SpringerBriefs in Criminolc

For further volumes:
http://www.springer.com/series/10159

Ramón Spaaij

Understanding Lone Wolf Terrorism

Global Patterns, Motivations and Prevention

Springer

Dr. Ramón Spaaij
School of Social Sciences
La Trobe University
Melbourne, VIC
Australia
e-mail: r.spaaij@latrobe.edu.au

ISSN 2192-8533
ISBN 978-94-007-2980-3
DOI 10.1007/978-94-007-2981-0
Springer Dordrecht Heidelberg London New York

ISSN 2192-8541 (eBook)
ISBN 978-94-007-2981-0 (eBook)

Library of Congress Control Number: 2011944127

Printed on acid-free paper

Springer is part of Springer Science+Business Media (www.springer.com)

Acknowledgments

I would like to thank Myriam Poort, Editorial Director Social Sciences at Springer Science+Business Media, who invited me to write this volume. I am grateful to Dennis de Hoog and Marieke Matthijs for their collegiality, stimulating discussions and incisive comments on an earlier version of this publication. Marieke Matthijs also provided invaluable research assistance for one of the case studies. My inspiring conversations with Astrid Meland have also helped shape some of the ideas presented in this volume. I am very grateful to Maryann Martin for her expert editing. Part of the research on which this volume is based was conducted for the European Commission Sixth Framework Program project *Transnational Terrorism, Security and the Rule of Law* (TTSRL). Information on the TTSRL project can be found at http://www.transnationalterrorism.eu. I thank Taylor & Francis for permission to include material from "The Enigma of Lone Wolf Terrorism: An Assessment", *Studies in Conflict & Terrorism*, 33 (2010): 854–870. This article has been updated, fully revised and expanded into book-length form for publication.

Contents

Chapter 1
Introduction

> I attempted to kill many. I followed through with many actions that I hoped would either terrorize and coerce others to change their ways… or halt their actions through death. … I am caged now because of potential, and because of opinion. … Though I began with no money, and little or no knowledge of strategic warfare, I feel that I successfully challenged an evil government and those who oppress children and Christians in this nation.
>
> – Anti-abortion activist Paul Ross Evans [31][1]

> While terrorism needs to be condemned in the strongest possible terms, mere condemnation will not lead to a better understanding of the phenomenon, which needs to be analysed in all its forms and manifestations. To try to understand terrorism – a form of action that often appears absurd when one looks only at the nature of the uninvolved and innocent victims and not at the intended target audiences – does not involve acceptance.
>
> – Alex P. Schmid [1, p. 412]

The tragedy that unfolded in Norway on the afternoon of 22 July 2011 has put acts of terrorism carried out by single individuals squarely on the political and media agendas of several western societies. Moreover, it has generated serious reflection on the threat posed by "lone wolves" and the capacity of existing counterterrorism measures to interdict this type of attack. On that fateful day, an improvised explosive device hidden in a car was detonated at the centre of the executive government quarter in Oslo, killing eight people. Two hours after the explosion, a gunman disguised as a police officer opened fire on a summer camp organized by the Norwegian Labour Party's youth association AUF on the island of Utøya, located 32 kilometers outside of Oslo. The shooting eventually claimed 69 lives, raising the total death toll to 77. The suspect, 32-year-old Anders Behring Breivik, confessed to committing both attacks and has been charged under Norwegian criminal law for acts of terrorism. The charges include the destabilization of vital functions of society, including government, and causing serious fear in the population [2].

---

[1] Paul Ross Evans was sentenced to 40 years in prison for attempting to bomb the Austin Women's Health Center in the United States in 2007.

R. Spaaij, *Understanding Lone Wolf Terrorism*, SpringerBriefs in Criminology,
DOI: 10.1007/978-94-007-2981-0_1, © The Author(s) 2012

Shortly before the 22 July 2011 attacks on Oslo and the island of Utøya, Breivik posted a 1,517-page manifesto on the Internet in which he gave a detailed description and diary of his operations and justified the massacre as "necessary" to save Norway and Europe from Muslim immigrants and specifically to punish his country's political establishment for embracing multiculturalism [3]. It is believed that Breivik acted completely on his own, despite some suggestions—including by Breivik himself—that he may have been part of a larger extremist network [4, 5].

In the wake of the attacks in Norway, European security officials emphasized that the issue of lone wolf terrorism—terrorist attacks carried out individually and independently from established terrorist organizations or networks—required increasing attention, while at the same time warning that more traditional terrorism threats should not be neglected [6]. Indeed, the European Police Chiefs Convention [7, p. 1] concludes that "the changing dynamics in our societies, together with technological advances, may encourage isolated, disaffected individuals to turn into violent extremists, to the extreme of becoming 'lone wolf' terrorists". According to Europol [8, p. 15], radicalized individuals "are often hard to identify as they act alone and their activities can be unpredictable and difficult to prevent".

The Norwegian tragedy has also led non-European governments to reflect on the threat of lone wolf terrorism on their territory. For example, Australian Security Intelligence Organisation (ASIO) Director-General David Irvine [9, p. 4] states that "what happened in Norway should remind our community that threats to our security may come not from one or two sources, but many", including solo actor terrorists. Irvine [9] goes on to argue that the most likely form of terrorist attack in Australia in the near future would be low-cost, locally financed, involve minimal training and a short planning cycle, and use weapons fabricated or sourced from readily available materials that were unlikely to arouse suspicion.

It is in the United States, however, that lone wolf terrorism has been considered a significant and ongoing security threat for some time now [10–12], with the mass shootings at the military complex of Fort Hood in November 2009, which killed 13 and wounded 43, reinforcing this perception. As FBI Director Robert Mueller III [13, p. 3] states, "the threat from single individuals sympathetic or affiliated with Al Qaeda, acting without external support or surrounding conspiracies, is increasing". In similar terms to Europol, Mueller notes that these individuals are particularly hard to identify before they strike. In 2010, CIA Director Leon Panetta stresses the danger of terrorists acting alone by asserting that "it's the lone wolf strategy that I think we have to pay attention to as the main threat to this country" [14].

United States President Barack Obama and Homeland Security Secretary Janet Napolitano have recently voiced similar concerns. Obama asserts that a lone wolf terrorist attack in the United States is now more likely than a major coordinated effort like the 9/11 attacks:

> The risk that we're especially concerned over right now is the lone wolf terrorist, somebody with a single weapon being able to carry out wide-scale massacres of the sort that we saw in Norway recently. You know, when you've got one person who is deranged or driven by a hateful ideology, they can do a lot of damage, and it's a lot harder to trace those lone wolf operators [15].

In a similar vein, US Homeland Security Secretary Napolitano calls lone wolf terrorist attacks "the most challenging" from a law enforcement perspective, "because by definition they're not conspiring. They're not using the phones, the computer networks, or any—they're not talking with others any other way that we might get some inkling about what is being planned" [16]. A year earlier, a Homeland Security report describes "lone wolves and small terrorist cells embracing violent rightwing extremist ideology" as "the most dangerous domestic terrorism threat in the United States" [17, p. 7].

A recurrent theme in statements from law enforcement and security agencies on lone wolf terrorism (and terrorism in general) is the opportunities new information and communication technologies (ICTs) afford to actual or would-be terrorists. For example, Irvine [9, p. 1] argues that "the rampant use of the Internet, the democratisation of communication, has resulted in new and effective means for individuals to propagate and absorb unfettered ideas and information and to be radicalised—literally, in their lounge rooms". The Internet allows extremist messages to be communicated and terrorist skills and expertise to be shared and developed with relative ease [18], which may result in a rise in individualized terrorism that is unconnected to known terrorist groups and hard to foresee and prevent [19]. Anders Breivik's vigorous use of the Internet in the preparatory phase of his alleged attacks and, subsequently, in spreading his message to a global audience, is a case in point. At the same time, however, cutting-edge technologies (including the use of the Internet) have become an integral part of counterterrorism and intelligence operations (e.g. [19, 20]).

How, then, have scholars of terrorism and counterterrorism addressed the issue of lone wolf terrorism? Overall, there exists a significant discrepancy between the recent political and media attention on lone wolf terrorism on the one hand, and scientific investigation of this phenomenon on the other. Systematic research into lone wolf terrorism has been rare. Terrorism is usually viewed as essentially a collective, organized activity and, consequently, scholars focus predominantly on group dynamics and collective socialization to explain individual pathways into terrorism. Social psychological explanations of terrorism tend to emphasize the influence of charismatic leaders, ideological training and indoctrination, moral disengagement, in-group solidarity, conformity and obedience, depersonalization, social closure, and other factors relating to organizational and interpersonal processes (e.g. [21–26]). In this context, Moghaddam [27, p. 166] posits:

> Commitment to the terrorist cause strengthens as the new recruit is socialized into the traditions, methods, and goals of the organization.... [C]onformity and obedience will be very high in the cells of the terrorist organization, where the cell leader represents a strong authority figure and where nonconformity, disobedience, and disloyalty receive the harshest punishments.

In a similar vein, Crenshaw [28] argues that terrorism is the result of a gradual growth of commitment both to political objectives *and* to a group. For Crenshaw [28, p. 103], "the psychological relationships within a group—the interplay of commitment, risk, solidarity, loyalty, guilt, revenge, and isolation—discourage members from altering the course they have taken".

While interpretations of this kind are helpful in understanding collective forms of terrorism, it remains unclear how and to what extent dominant explanations of terrorism apply to the actions of solo actors. Hoffman [29, pp. 16–17] makes the important point that:

> … the traditional way of understanding terrorism and looking at terrorists based on organizational definitions and attributes in some cases is no longer relevant. Increasingly, lone individuals with no connection with or formal ties to established or identifiable terrorist organizations are rising up to engage in violence.

Hoffman's [29] comment points to the need for a better understanding of the nature and causes of lone wolf terrorism, a need that is underlined by the dearth of in-depth analysis on the subject. For example, while a great deal has been learned about how individuals become radicalized in groups—ranging from hierarchical organizations to decentralized or "homegrown" cells—much less has been ascertained about how lone wolves, who by definition act on their own, become radicalized to the point where they put their radical beliefs into practice through the use of violence. Although the vast majority of persons who have been arrested for terrorism offences appear to be members of, or in some other way connected to, established or identifiable terrorist groups, a small but significant proportion (roughly 2%) has been identified as lone individuals [30]. As will be seen, whilst lone wolf terrorist incidents account for only a very small percentage of the total number of terrorist attacks, the number of this type of attack has been on the rise in recent decades.

In order to fill this knowledge void, the present volume seeks to produce an in-depth understanding of lone wolf terrorism. It focuses on six key dimensions of lone wolf terrorism, each of which refers to a series of questions or themes that typically feature in political, media and academic debates following an act of lone wolf terrorism. These dimensions are:

- *Definition*: What is lone wolf terrorism? How is it different from other forms of terrorism, if at all? Is there a difference between a lone wolf terrorist and a lone assassin? What are the limitations of distinguishing lone wolf terrorism as a separate category of terrorism?
- *Incidence and evolution*: How common is lone wolf terrorism? How deadly is it? How is lone wolf terrorism distributed geographically? Has its incidence changed over time?
- *Motivations and ideologies*: What are the motivational patterns of lone wolf terrorists? Which ideologies do they adhere to?
- *Influences and radicalization*: Under what sociological and psychological conditions do individuals engage in lone wolf terrorism? What are the links between lone wolf terrorists and other terrorist subjects or extremist communities? How are these individuals brought to the point where they see themselves as bearers of the responsibility for violent actions?

- *Modus operandi*: How are acts of lone wolf terrorism planned and carried out? What are lone wolves' preferred weapons of attack? Who or what are the main targets of lone wolf terrorism?
- *Responses*: Why is it so difficult to prevent lone wolf terrorist attacks? How do governments respond to lone wolf terrorism? What are the effects of these responses, and what lessons can be learned from them?

In conjunction, these dimensions cover the *who, what, why, how, when* and *where* of lone wolf terrorism. Another important element that is explored in this volume is the forms that counterterrorism takes, and how these forms affect lone wolf terrorist activity.

The content of this volume is structured according to these dimensions, with each chapter examining one key dimension of lone wolf terrorism and the corresponding questions. The volume proceeds by succinctly outlining in Chap. 2 the data collection and analysis methods used. Following this methodological note, Chap. 3 seeks to conceptualize and contextualize lone wolf terrorism, providing a number of definitions and discussing the key definitional elements of lone wolf terrorism as well as the complexities and limits of categorizing it as a distinct type of terrorist and criminal activity. In Chap. 4, the attention shifts to the historical context of lone wolf terrorism. This chapter also examines the incidence and geographical distribution of lone wolf terrorist attacks as well as the patterns of continuity and change therein. Chapter 5 analyzes the motivations and ideologies of lone wolf terrorists, highlighting the diversity of radical political, ideological and religious beliefs that may inspire their actions as well as the role of personal grievances. The discussion of the motivational patterns displayed by these lone wolf terrorists continues in Chap. 6, which shifts the focus toward other factors and influences that affect the violent radicalization of these individuals. Following on from the examination of radicalization processes, Chap. 7 addresses the modus operandi of lone wolf terrorists, with a particular emphasis on the selection of targets and weapons as well as the planning and execution of these attacks. In Chap. 8, the attention shifts to the ways in which governments and communities respond to lone wolf terrorism, analyzing a range of legal, repressive and conciliatory responses that have been taken to minimize this type of terrorism. The final chapter, "Conclusion and outlook", draws together and reflects on the main findings and insights of this volume.

References

1. Schmid AP (2004) Terrorism: the definitional problem. Case Western Reserve J Int Law 36:375–419
2. BBC (2011) Norway: Anders Behring Breivik claims 'two more cells'. BBC News, 25 July. http://www.bbc.co.uk/news/world-europe-14280210. Accessed 26 July 2011
3. Breivik A (2011) 2083: A European declaration of independence. http://www.washingtonpost.com/r/2010-2019/WashingtonPost/2011/07/24/National-Politics/Graphics/2083+-+A+European+Declaration+of+Independence.pdf. Accessed 26 July 2011

4. Erlanger S (2011) Norway suspect denies guilt and suggests he did not act alone. The New York Times, New York (25 July)
5. Millar L (2011) I didn't act alone, Norway attacker tells court. ABC News, 26 July. http://www.abc.net.au/news/2011-07-25/norway-attacks-suspect-arrives-in-court/2809930. Accessed 27 July 2011
6. Vogel T (2011) EU considers response to Norway attacks. The European Voice, 25 July. http://www.europeanvoice.com/article/2011/july/eu-ponders-response-to-norway-attacks/71732.aspx. Accessed 30 July 2011
7. European Police Chiefs Convention (2011) Counter terrorism working group conclusions. Europol, The Hague https://www.europol.europa.eu/sites/default/files/publications/epcccounterterrorismconclusions.pdf Accessed 15 August 2011
8. Europol (2011) TE-SAT 2011: EU terrorism situation and trend report. Europol, Hague
9. Irvine D (2011) Australia's security outlook. Presented at the Security in Government Conference, National Convention Centre, Canberra, 26 July
10. Thomas J (1999) New face of terror crimes: 'Lone wolf' weaned on hate. The New York Times, New York (16 August 1)
11. Johnston D, Risen J (2003) Lone terrorists may strike in the US agencies warn. The New York Times, New York (23 February 15)
12. Marks A (2003) Lone wolves' pose explosive terror threat. The Christian Science Monitor, Boston (27 May 2)
13. Mueller R (2003) War on terrorism: Testimony of Robert S. Mueller, III, Director, FBI, before the Select Committee on Intelligence of the United States Senate, Washington, 11 February 2003. http://www.intelcenter.com/resource/2003/mueller.pdf. Accessed 6 June 2007
14. Anonymous (2010) Intelligence officials warn attempted Al Qaeda attack months away. FOXNews.com. 2 February. http://www.foxnews.com/politics/2010/02/02/intelligence-officials-warn-attempted-al-qaeda-attack-months-away#ixzz1XiqcKyiw. Accessed 4 July 2010
15. CNN (2011) Obama: biggest terror fear is the lone wolf. CNN Situation Room, 16 August. http://security.blogs.cnn.com/2011/08/16/obama-biggest-terror-fear-is-the-lone-wolf/. Accessed 18 August 2011
16. Kerley D (2010) Homeland security: more 'lone wolves' circulating in US. ABC News, 6 March. http://abcnews.go.com/WN/homeland-security-lone-wolves-circulating-us/story?id=10030050. Accessed 16 August 2011
17. Department of Homeland Security (2009) Rightwing extremism: current economic and political climate fueling resurgence in radicalization and recruitment. DHS, Washington
18. Weimann G (2006) Terror on the internet. United States Institute of Peace Press, Washington
19. Lia B (2005) Globalisation and the future of terrorism: patterns and predictions. Routledge, London
20. Castells M (2010) The information age: economy, society and culture, 2nd edn. Wiley-Blackwell, Oxford (volumes I-III)
21. Post JM (1998) Terrorist psycho-logic: terrorist behavior as a product of psychological forces. In: Reich W (ed) Origins of terrorism. Woodrow Wilson Center Press, Washington, pp 25–41
22. Bandura A (1998) Mechanisms of moral disengagement. In: Reich W (ed) Origins of terrorism. Woodrow Wilson Center Press, Washington, pp 161–191
23. Hudson R (1999) The sociology and psychology of terrorism: Who becomes a terrorist and why. Federal Research Division, Library of Congress, Washington
24. Horgan J (2005) The psychology of terrorism. Routledge, London
25. Forest JJ (ed) (2006) The making of a terrorist: Recruitment, training, and root causes. Praeger Security International, Westport
26. Mullins S (2009) Parallels between crime and terrorism: a social psychological perspective. Stud Conflict Terrorism 32(9):811–830
27. Moghaddam F (2005) The staircase to terrorism: a psychological exploration. Am Psychol 60(2):161–169

28. Crenshaw M (2003) The causes of terrorism. In: Jr Kegley CW (ed) The new global terrorism: characteristics, causes, controls. Prentice Hall, Upper Saddle River, pp 92–105
29. Hoffman B (2003) Al Qaeda, trends in terrorism, and future potentialities: an assessment. RAND, Santa Monica
30. Hewitt C (2003) Understanding terrorism in America: from the Klan to al Qaeda. Routledge, New York
31. Evans PR (n.d.) Methodical terrorism: How and why. http://www.armyofgod.com/POCPaulRossEvansMethodicalTerrorism.html. Accessed 12 August 2011

Chapter 2
A Note on Method

The comparative analysis presented in this volume draws on existing literature and empirical data to provide an overview and critical discussion of what we presently know and do not know about lone wolf terrorism. Due to the dearth of systematic academic research on the subject, extensive empirical data are used to enable a more in-depth analysis of the key dimensions of lone wolf terrorism. The bulk of these data was initially collected and analyzed as part of the European Commission Sixth Framework Program project *Transnational Terrorism, Security and the Rule of Law* (TTSRL), a three-year research project (2006–2009) that aimed to help Europe better understand terrorism. TTSRL focused on a broad range of terrorism-related subjects, including radicalization, the relation with the media, counterterrorism, theoretical background, academic discourse and practical case studies.

2.1 Chronology of Lone Wolf Terrorism in 15 Countries, 1968–2010

The data used here derive from multiple complementary sources. In order to assess the incidence, evolution and nature of lone wolf terrorism, I have compiled a database of all terrorist attacks carried out by lone individuals between 1 January 1968 and 31 December 2010 in the 15 countries that are covered in the TTSRL research project.[2] These countries are: United Kingdom, Germany, France, Spain, Italy, Poland, The Netherlands, Denmark, Sweden, Czech Republic, Portugal, Russia, Australia, Canada and United States. The database is primarily based on an analysis of the Global Terrorism Database (GTD) and the RAND-MIPT Terrorism Knowledge Base (TKB). All recorded incidents for the period 1968–2007 were cross-checked in both the GTD and the TKB. Because the TKB ceased operations on 31 March 2008, I used only the GTD for the period 2008–2010. The GTD

[2] The initial database of lone wolf terrorism compiled by the author in 2007 [1, 2] contained significant gaps, most of which have subsequently been resolved.

R. Spaaij, *Understanding Lone Wolf Terrorism*, SpringerBriefs in Criminology,
DOI: 10.1007/978-94-007-2981-0_2,

contains by far the largest number of domestic and international terrorism events compared to any of the other existing terrorism data sets, including the TKB [3].

Information in the GTD and TKB is drawn from open-source materials, such as electronic news archives, existing data sets, secondary source materials (e.g. books and journals) and legal documents. All information contained in these databases reflects what is reported in those sources. The GTD database developers seek to corroborate each piece of information among multiple independent open sources, and require that each case included be verified by at least two separate sources. However, they make no further claims as to the veracity of this information [4]. In developing and cross-checking the database of lone wolf terrorism using the GTD and TKB, only those cases were considered in which two criteria were met: (1) the act must be aimed at attaining a political, ideological or religious goal; and (2) there must be evidence of an intention to coerce, intimidate, or convey some other message to a larger audience than the immediate victims. Attacks that were attempted but not successfully carried out were included in the analysis.

The GTD and TKB have serious weaknesses, however, that should be kept in mind when interpreting the data. First and foremost, by relying on data culled from open sources, the data sets are likely to be biased toward the most newsworthy forms of terrorism. In particular, "it is reasonable to conclude that media accounts will be more likely to miss attacks that were averted by authorities, that were unsuccessful, or that happened in regions of the world with less media coverage" [3, p. 188]. It is certain that some potential terrorist attacks never came to the attention of the media and are thus excluded. This issue is taken up in Chap. 4 in the discussion of the "hidden figure" of lone wolf terrorism. Second, the GTD and TKB (like all other open-source data sets) lack information on important issues associated with terrorism incidents. Specifically, three complicating factors were encountered during the research:

- In several cases the open sources are unable to identify the perpetrators; without this information, it is very difficult to accurately classify incidents as lone wolf terrorism. The following example from the TKB illustrates this issue: "Denmark, 15 September 1985, Unknown group. Coinciding with the Jewish New Year, a bomb exploded at an Israeli travel agency in Copenhagen. No one claimed responsibility for the blast. Twelve people were injured" (previously accessible at www.mipt.org). The GTD contains similar cases, for instance: "07/03/2007: Khavazh Daurbekov, deputy mayor of Karabulak town in the Ingushetia Republic of Russia, was assassinated near his home by an unknown gunman. No claim of responsibility was reported" (http://www.start.umd.edu/gtd/search/IncidentSummary.aspx?gtdid=200707030010).
- At times a known extremist group is suspected but no conclusive evidence is presented to verify the type of perpetrator (individual or collective; affiliated or unaffiliated). Consider the following example from the GTD: "12/29/2010: On Wednesday night, in Lombardy, Varese, Italy, two small improvised explosive devices detonated outside the political headquarters of the Northern League party. The building and some furniture were damaged but there were no

casualties reported. No group claimed responsibility but Informal Anarchic Federation militants *were suspected* to have carried out the attack" (http://www.start.umd.edu/gtd/search/IncidentSummary.aspx?gtdid=201012290003; emphasis added).

- In some instances, time and deeper exploration uncovers links to broader networks which indicate that a terrorist attack may not have been an instance of lone wolf terrorism [5]. The GTD and TKB do not always follow up and record this subsequent information. In a number of cases the GTD and TKB do relate seemingly individual acts of terrorism to broader extremist organizations. The alleged connection between Richard Reid and Al Qaeda is a case in point (http://www.start.umd.edu/gtd/search/IncidentSummary.aspx?gtdid=200112220002). Reid attempted to detonate explosives in his shoes on a flight en route to Miami from Paris, on 22 December 2001. After several failed attempts Reid was restrained by passengers. Reid, who converted to Islam while in prison, was reportedly trained by Al Qaeda [6, 7]. Where perpetrators can be tied to an established or identifiable extremist group (even if such a connection remains inconclusive), they have been excluded from the list. For example, Alexei Korshunov, the accused killer of court judge Eduard Chuvashov in Moscow on 12 April 2010, is reportedly a member of the neo-Nazi group OB-88 whose members include suspects in other high-profile murders of Russian left-wing activists and officials [8, 9].

Taking into account these limitations as well as the difficulties associated with defining lone wolf terrorism (see Chap. 3), it is clear that some degree of arbitrariness inevitably remains present in labelling an act "lone wolf terrorism".

The recorded incidents of lone wolf terrorism were corroborated through an analysis of media reports, security reports, and chronologies and encyclopedias of terrorism (e.g. [10–13]). A number of ambiguous incidents were excluded due to either profound confusion about the identity of the perpetrator, the perpetrator's alleged connections with a terrorist group, or the absence of a "terrorist purpose" (see Chap. 3).[3] In a few cases it has not been possible to trace the exact circumstances of an attack, which resulted in their exclusion from the database. The analysis of alternative sources also led to the inclusion into the database of lone wolf terrorism incidents that were not recorded in the GTD and TKB.

The process of cross-checking resulted in the exclusion from the database of a number of recent violent acts by stand-alone individuals that were carried out for reasons of personal motivation, or simply with criminal intent. Four such incidents deserve mention here because they are sometimes wrongly classified as lone wolf terrorism. The first incident is the mass shooting on the campus of Virginia Tech

---

[3] The arson attack on a house inhabited by refugees in Lübeck, Germany, in January 1996 is a case in point. The attack killed ten people and injured 38. Investigators suspected Safwan Eid, a Lebanese national living in the house. Others claimed that it was the work of neo-Nazis and that the accused was in fact a victim. Eid was twice acquitted due to lack of evidence. The case may be reopened due to new evidence that four neo-Nazis were the perpetrators of the attack.

on 16 April 2007, in which 33 students, including the shooter, lost their lives. In a series of videos broadcast days after the shootings, the perpetrator, Seung-Hui Cho, revealed himself as a deeply disturbed individual obsessed with violence and harboring profound and unexplained grievances, apparently against his fellow students [14]. The second event, also in the United States, involved a hostage situation at the Discovery Communications headquarters in Silver Spring, Maryland, on 1 September 2010. The perpetrator, James Lee, was reportedly motivated by his disapproval of the Discovery network's television programming. In the manifesto he posted on the Internet, Lee laid out demands for the network to change its programming. Lee was eventually shot to death by police snipers; all three hostages were freed unharmed.

The third incident took place on 1 May 2009 in Apeldoorn, the Netherlands, where eight people were killed, including the driver, when 38-year-old Karst Tates drove his car into a crowd of civilians attending a festival. The intended target of the attack was a bus carrying the Dutch royal family. Tates left no note or any other indication of his motivations; it is therefore not possible to determine with any certainty a political motive. The fourth incident involved the airplane hijacking at Moscow's Domodedovo airport on 29 July 2010. Thirty-nine-year-old Magomed Patiyev held 105 passengers hostage and demanded a meeting with law enforcement officials and journalists, claiming to have valuable information about a bombing that occurred earlier that year. Patiyev was unarmed and made no direct threats during the standoff [15, 16]. As noted, all four incidents outlined above were excluded from the database due to the presumed absence of a political, religious or social goal.

The database of lone wolf terrorism compiled by the author comprises a total of 88 lone wolves who in conjunction have committed a total of (at least) 198 terrorist attacks in the 15 countries under study between 1968 and 2010. The details of these cases can be found in the Appendix. Only two perpetrators were identified as being female (American anti-abortion activist Rachelle Shannon and radicalized British Islamist Roshonara Choudhry), which means that almost all lone wolf terrorists in the sample are men. Specific details from this database are referred to throughout the text.

2.2 Qualitative Case Studies

In addition to developing a database of lone wolf terrorism, five cases were studied in depth to obtain a deeper understanding of the phenomenon. These cases are used here to analyze the nature and key dimensions of lone wolf terrorism. The case studies were selected on the basis of their diversity in terms of (a) the number of fatalities and injuries, (b) the time span (ranging from a single attack to a prolonged terrorist campaign), and (c) the geographical location of the attacks. The case studies are based on an analysis of writings and statements by the perpetrators, media reports (print and online), police and court transcripts, psychological

Table 2.1 Lone wolf terrorism case studies

Name	Location	Time span	Fatalities/injuries
Theodore Kaczynski	United States	1978–1995	3/23
Franz Fuchs	Austria	1993–1996	4/15
Yigal Amir	Israel	Single attack in 1995	1/0
David Copeland	United Kingdom	Two-week spree in 1999	3/129
Volkert van der Graaf	Netherlands	Single attack in 2002	1/0

and psychiatric evaluations, and relevant literature. It is important to stress that these cases are by no means exhaustive or representative of all known acts of lone wolf terrorism, but are used in an explorative way to gauge some of the key features of the phenomenon. The five cases exemplify many differences in the political or ideological backgrounds of the perpetrators, their radicalization, targets and modus operandi, which highlight the absence of a single, standardized profile of a lone wolf terrorist [2, 17]. The cases are summarized in Table 2.1.

Finally, this analysis of lone wolf terrorism draws on the writings of a number of other, more recent lone wolves, including the accused Norwegian terrorist Anders Behring Breivik and American anti-abortion activist Paul Ross Evans. First, however, in the next chapter lone wolf terrorism will be defined and conceptualized.

References

1. Spaaij R (2007) Lone-wolf terrorism. Report for the European Commission Sixth Framework program Transnational Terrorism, Security and the Rule of Law. COT Institute for Safety, Security and Crisis Management, The Hague
2. Spaaij R (2010) The enigma of lone wolf terrorism: an assessment. Stud Conflict Terror 33(9):854–870
3. LaFree G, Dugan L (2007) Introducing the global terrorism database. Terror Political Violence 19:181–204
4. Global Terrorism Database (2011) Data collection methodology. http://www.start.umd.edu/gtd/using-gtd/. Accessed 12 Aug 2011
5. Pantucci R (2011) A typology of lone wolves: preliminary analysis of lone Islamist terrorists. ICSR, London
6. Ressa M (2003) Sources: Reid is al Qaeda operative. CNN, 6 December. http://articles.cnn.com/2003-01-30/world/reid.alqaeda_1_qaeda-khalden-rohan gunaratna?_s=PM:WORLD. Accessed 4 Sept 2011
7. Elliott M (2002) The shoe bomber's world. Time 25:18–23 (February)
8. SOVA Center for Information and Analysis (2011) Investigators name suspect in murder of Moscow judge. SOVA News Release, 1 April. http://www.sova-center.ru/en/xenophobia/news-releases/2011/04/d21295/. Accessed 20 Aug 2011
9. Anonymous (2011) I won't tell you just yet, but perhaps I'll tell you later. *Novaya Gazeta*, 4 April. http://en.novayagazeta.ru/data/2011/033/00.html. Accessed 20 Aug 2011
10. Mickolus EF (1980) Transnational terrorism: a chronology of events, 1968–1979. Greenwood Press, Westport

11. Branum TL (2001) Aviation security in the new century. Federalist Society for Law and Public Policy Studies, Washington
12. Kushner H (2003) Encyclopedia of terrorism. Sage, Thousand Oaks
13. Hewitt C (2005) Political violence and terrorism in modern America. Praeger Security International, Westport
14. BBC (2007) Loner filled with anger and spite. BBC News, 19 April
15. Eremenko A (2010) Passenger detained after airport standoff. The Moscow Times, 30 July. http://www.themoscowtimes.com/news/article/passenger-detained-after-airport-standoff/411348.html. Accessed 20 Aug 2011
16. Anonymous (2010) Plane 'hijacker' had terror tip for Putin. The Moscow Times, 2 August. http://www.themoscowtimes.com/news/article/plane-hijacker-had-terror-tip-for-putin/411436.html. Accessed 20 Aug 2011
17. Bakker E, de Graaf B (2010) Lone wolves: how to prevent this phenomenon? International Centre for Counter-Terrorism, The Hague

Chapter 3
Definition of Lone Wolf Terrorism

3.1 The Social Construction of Terrorism

Terrorism is a contested and intensely political concept, and there is neither academic nor policy consensus on its definition. As Schmid [1, p. 380] notes, "the term is used promiscuously for such a wide range of manifestations ... that one wonders whether it is a unitary concept". Attempts at consensus on terrorism [e.g. 2] come at the price of both a serious reduction of complexity [1] and the (inadvertent) concealment of issues of power that are centrally implicated in any definition of terrorism. One of the most significant contributions to our understanding of terrorism is the realization that terrorism is a social construct. Indeed, terrorism is not a given in the real world, but "an interpretation of events and their presumed causes" [3, p. 491]. Such interpretation is not an unbiased attempt to depict truth; rather, it is a conscious effort to "manipulate perceptions to promote certain interests at the expense of others" [3, p. 491]. Definitions of terrorism typically reflect the interests of those who do the defining, and in many social conflicts the government and related agencies (e.g. the security industry) are the "primary definer" [4] and hold *de facto* "definition power" [5]. The recent government statements on lone wolf terrorism discussed in Chap. 1, are an example of such definition power. In this context, it has been demonstrated how fear of terrorism is fuelled by those with vested interests for their own purposes [6, 7].

The definition question is thus not simply a matter of academic nit-picking. On the contrary, it is intimately linked to issues of (de)legitimization, criminalization and moral justification of responses [8, 9]. One major issue of contention is whether the term "terrorism" should apply to the actions of state bodies in the same way that it applies to the actions of non-state actors. Throughout history, terrorism practiced by states or governments and their agents and allies, most notably against civilians and political, ethnic or religious opposition groups, has been far deadlier and far more prevalent than anti-state terrorism [10–13]. Importantly, the Global Terrorism Database (GTD) referred to in the previous chapter lacks information on state terrorism due to its focus on sub-national perpetrators, even though the database developers recognize that more information is

R. Spaaij, *Understanding Lone Wolf Terrorism*, SpringerBriefs in Criminology,
DOI: 10.1007/978-94-007-2981-0_3, © The Author(s) 2012

needed on this matter [14]. The issue of state terrorism is less relevant for the present purpose because, as shown below, acts of lone wolf terrorism are by definition not committed or organized by agencies of the state.

A second key definitional dilemma is whether or not (and, if so, how) one should differentiate between acts of terrorism and the rights of peoples to self-determination and to combat foreign occupation [1]. In this context, a well-known aphorism is that one man's terrorist is another man's freedom fighter [15]. In reflecting on this issue and on the socially constructed nature of terrorism more generally, Sluka [16, p. 23] argues that to seek an understanding of terrorism and its causes, social scientists:

> … must apply a critical perspective to the way in which élites, governments, the media and other academics employ the concept of terrorism, must energetically criticize those who subvert the idea for propaganda purposes, and must ensure that we are objective, empirical, and honest in our own use of the concept.

3.2 What is Lone Wolf Terrorism?

A critical discussion of general terrorism definitions lies beyond the scope of this volume. Instead, the focus is on conceptualizing how *lone wolf* terrorism may be different from other types of terrorism and political violence, taking into account Sluka's [16] important recommendation. Definition of the term "lone wolf" is imperative because it is often misused or used imprecisely [17]. Thus, the term "lone wolf" is used here to distinguish terrorist activities carried out by lone individuals from those carried out on the part of terrorist organizations or state bodies. The element of terrorism highlighted in this distinction is the *subjects* of terrorist acts (individuals, terrorist groups, state bodies) rather than, for example, their specific political, ideological or religious aims [18].

The most frequently cited definition of a "lone wolf" person is the definition provided by Burton and Stewart [17]: "A lone wolf is a person who acts on his or her own without orders from—or even connections to—an organization". They stress that a lone wolf is distinct from a "sleeper operative", in that a sleeper is an operative who infiltrates the targeted society or organization and then remains dormant until a group or organization orders them into action. In contrast, a lone wolf is "a standalone operative who by his very nature is embedded in the targeted society and is capable of self-activation at any time" [17].

Elsewhere I propose a similar, albeit narrower, definition that highlights three key features of lone wolf terrorists: they (a) operate individually, (b) do not belong to an organized terrorist group or network, and (c) their modi operandi are conceived and directed by the individual without any direct outside command or hierarchy [19]. In following this definition, my position differs from that of Hoffman [20, pp. 42–43] as expressed in his book *Inside Terrorism*, in which he argues that "to qualify as terrorism, violence must be perpetrated by some organizational entity with at least some conspiratorial structure and identifiable chain of command beyond a single individual acting on his or her own". However, by definition, lone wolf terrorism takes place in the absence of such an organizational entity. Hoffman's [21] later work explicitly recognizes this where he notes that lone individuals with no connection with or formal ties to established or identifiable terrorist organizations are rising up to engage in political violence.

The above definitions direct our attention to four key issues that should be taken into account in distinguishing lone wolf terrorism from other types of terrorist and criminal activity. First, in terrorism research and policy the term "lone wolf" is typically used in ways that deviate from the biological meaning of the term. Wolf biology shows that whilst wolf (*canis lupus*) populations are composed of packs and lone wolves, packs form the basic units of a population. Lone wolves are those wolves which have dispersed from packs and are travelling alone either to start their own packs or join existing packs [22]. While these lone animals strive to maintain a low profile while travelling, most wolves are only temporarily alone. Lone wolf terrorists, on the other hand, do not necessarily seek to establish their own group or join an existing group, and may be permanently disconnected from group-actor terrorism. Notwithstanding these deviations, however, the above definitions of lone wolf terrorism resonate with the biological meaning of the term in their emphasis on those individuals who do not belong to a terrorist group (i.e. to a "pack").

As will be seen, the lone wolf terrorist is typically someone who acts out of a strong political, ideological or religious conviction, carefully plans his or her actions, and may successfully hide his or her operations from those around them (i.e. lead some kind of "double life"). Although there is no consensus on its meaning, in this respect terrorism analysts' use of the term "lone wolf" tends to differ from how the term is utilized in studies of sex offenders, where the term is often applied to those sex predators who attack their victims in an impulsive, non-premeditated way [23], especially so-called "anger rapists" [24].[4] In recent years, the term "lone wolf" has also appeared in marketing and management literature, most notably in relation to team processes [25, 26].

A second key issue is that terrorist attacks carried out by couples or small cells do not, strictly speaking, qualify as lone wolf terrorism. This criterion excludes what Pantucci [27] somewhat confusingly calls a "lone wolf pack", that is, a small group of individuals who jointly radicalize. Decentralized grassroots operatives, such as those who were implicated in the homegrown terrorist attacks in London (7 July 2005) and Madrid (11 March 2004), had contact with a wider organization (e.g. a small autonomous cell or clique) and are not, by definition, lone wolves [17]. Homegrown terrorism essentially involves self-radicalized and self-activated groups—often autonomous cliques—without any direct contact with the terrorist networks from which they derive their inspiration [28]. Thus, in the case where a

---

[4] However, sexual offences clearly vary in terms of the level of planning and calculation involved [24].

lone wolf joins an established clique or cell, he or she ceases to be a lone wolf. This criterion also excludes certain high-profile terrorist attacks that are commonly ascribed to lone wolves, most notably the Oklahoma City bombing on 19 April 1995 which claimed 168 lives and wounded more than 500 people. Although the attack was carried out by an individual, Timothy McVeigh, his accomplice Terry Nichols played a considerable role in preparations for the attack [29–31], and there is evidence to suggest that McVeigh was connected to the Aryan Republican Army or other Christian fundamentalist groups [32]. It is important to note here that the term "lone wolf" is often erroneously deployed to provide easy explanations for what later turn out to be more complex terrorist attacks [27]. In this context, Jenkins [33] asserts that authorities have a tendency to suggest that a lone wolf or someone who is mentally unstable carried out the attack in order to avoid blame and accusations that they may have anticipated the incident and failed to act.

This issue is also directly relevant to the recent attacks in Norway. As noted in the Chap. 1, while the accused perpetrator Anders Breivik seems to have acted completely on his own and without any connection to an established or identifiable terrorist group, it has been speculated that he may be part of a larger cell of right-wing extremists. Although Breivik's [34] manifesto indicates that he planned and executed the attack as a lone wolf, it also suggests that he is linked to a group called the Pauperes commilitones Christi Templique Solomonici [Poor Fellow-Soldiers of Christ and of the Temple of Solomon (PCCTS)], also known as Knights Templar, a "European Christian military order" [34, p. 832] which seeks to encourage other lone wolves and small cells across Europe to carry out similar attacks. According to Breivik [34, p. 830], these "solo martyr cells" are "completely unknown to our enemies", and have "a minimal chance of being exposed". At his first court hearing on 25 July 2011, the accused Breivik repeated that he has "two more cells" working with him [35, 36]. Much like McVeigh, Breivik believes that his attack is the opening salvo in a wider campaign. It remains unclear, however, if this is a figment of his imagination or if Breivik has some factual basis for his belief that there are others like him planning attacks [37, 38]. Interestingly enough, Breivik's [34, p. 830] manifesto recommends that "optimally [lone wolves] should not have any affiliations to 'extremist networks' or to any extreme right wing movements for obvious reasons", that is, "to stay hidden". As shown in Chap. 5, Breivik's reference to a group is strongly reminiscent of Theodore Kaczynski's [39] statements that he was the leader of the Freedom Club (FC), fuelling the perception that a larger movement existed in the United States that thought as he did. Indeed, sections of Breivik's manifesto were copied from the manifesto of Kaczynski [40]. Franz Fuchs also claimed to be acting for a fictitious group, the Bavarian Liberation Army (e.g. [41, 42]).

A third main issue is that lone wolf terrorism should not be viewed as a distinctive category with regard to its political, ideological or religious bases. Lone wolf terrorists may identify or sympathize with larger extremist movements but, by definition, do not form part of these movements. As shown in Chap. 5, the spectrum of motivations and validations that has been described for terrorist organizations equally seems to apply to lone wolf terrorists, and many of the acts that appear to be solo ventures conducted by rogue activists actually have broader ideologies of validation and communities of belief behind them [30]. These ideologies thus extend beyond the scope of formal organization. Moreover, although lone wolf terrorists are by definition not tied to any established terrorist group, this is not to say that at one time they may not have been a member or affiliate of some type of extremist group; they may even have obtained some institutional training or support in the past. Their terrorist attack or campaign, however, results from solitary action during which the direct support of others, even those sympathetic to the cause, is absent. As will be seen in Chap. 6, there are interesting parallels between the accused Anders Breivik and British right-wing extremist David Copeland in this regard. Copeland, who carried out three bombings in 1999, was briefly a member of the British National Party (BNP) but left this party because it did not advocate violence [43, 44]. As an adolescent and young adult, Anders Breivik was a member of Norway's Progress Party (FpU) and its youth organization—describing it as a "moderate cultural conservative movement" [34, p. 1396]—and later possibly also participated in other right-wing organizations [45]. Similar to Copeland, Breivik [34, p. 1396] states that he left the Progress Party because it did not go far enough: "I eventually concluded that it would be impossible to change the system democratically and left conventional politics".

Finally, the boundaries of lone wolf terrorism are inevitably fuzzy. Some of the most striking political assassinations and mass murders in history were presumably carried out by lone individuals rather than groups [46], such as the assassinations of US Presidents James A. Garfield (1881), William McKinley Jr. (1901) and John F. Kennedy (1963). However, should these assassinations be regarded as acts of lone wolf terrorism? As with any act of terrorism, the intent or purpose of the violence is of central import in this consideration. Violence motivated exclusively by financial gain or personal vengeance does not constitute an act of terrorism because terrorist violence communicates a political message. As Jackson [47] points out, terrorism is not committed solely for the self-interest of the protagonist; instead, terrorist acts involve the use or threat of violence to create a wider culture of fear which can be used to advance political, religious or ideological causes. In short, terrorism has a political, rather than a merely personal or criminal, orientation (even though, in practice, political and criminal elements are often blurred; see [48]). While the violent act itself may be similar, the purpose or motivation is not [20]. Furthermore, from the terrorist's perspective the immediate target is usually of secondary import to the broader audience in which he or she seeks to install fear. As Crenshaw [49, p. 92] notes, the ends of terrorism "go beyond damaging an enemy's material resources. The victims or objects of terrorist attack represent an audience from whom terrorists seek a reaction". This key dimension of terrorism is well captured by Crelinsten [50, p. 6], who defines terrorism as violence "directed against one set of targets (the direct victims) in order to coerce compliance or to compel allegiance from a second set of targets (targets of demand) and to intimidate a wider audience (target of attention)".

What separates the actions of the lone wolf terrorist from those of the lone assassin, then, is the presence of a broader political, ideological or religious cause (however defined) that informs the actions of the former. In contrast, the lone assassin's goal is often "intrinsically idiosyncratic, completely egocentric and deeply personal" [20, p. 42]. In this vein, Burton and Stewart [17] distinguish between lone wolves and "lone nuts", that is, "mentally ill individuals motivated for other reasons", who "are not conducting politically motivated terrorist attacks". Turchie and Puckett [51] draw a similar distinction, arguing that one of the key characteristics of lone wolf terrorists is that although personal motivations for lethal violence may be present, accomplishing a larger political, ideological or religious goal is always a primary objective.

The question of whether acts of violence serve broader political, ideological or religious agendas leaves plenty of room for discussion. Assigning purposes and motives to acts of terrorism is inherently subjective and open to interpretation, especially when perpetrators do not claim responsibility for the attack [52]. Indeed, perpetrators' true motivations are rarely fully accessible or accurate [33]. These difficulties also apply to lone wolf terrorism. In many cases it is extremely difficult to determine the perpetrator's true motivation, even for those researchers who closely engage with the perpetrator. The purported motivation of Mir Aimal Kansi, a Pakistani immigrant to the United States who killed two CIA employees in 1993, is a noteworthy example. Terrorism expert Jessica Stern [53], who conducted an in-depth interview with Kansi, still has doubts as to whether he was motivated by anti-Americanism or by personal revenge. Stern [53, p. 181] stresses that "terrorists often use slogans of various kinds to mask their true motives".

The mass shootings at the military complex of Fort Hood in November 2009 raise similar questions. Army psychiatrist Major Nidal Malik Hasan killed 12 soldiers and one civilian and wounded 43 other people. Speculations about Hasan's motives are rife. Hasan reportedly held strong views in opposition to the wars in Iraq and Afghanistan and felt that Muslims should not be sent to fight other Muslims. Media reports suggest that Hasan engaged in e-mail correspondence with the Yemen-based radical cleric Anwar al-Awlaki, who is accused of spreading the Al Qaeda ideology. However, government officials claim that the messages "were largely questions about Islam, not expressions of militancy or hints of a plot", and that "the e-mail contacts were not a sign of a terrorist threat" [54, 55]. To date, it remains unclear whether the shootings were politically or religiously motivated. This confusion underlines the inherent difficulties in defining lone wolf terrorism. With these difficulties in mind, the next chapter examines the incidence and evolution of this phenomenon.

References

1. Schmid AP (2004) Terrorism: the definitional problem. Case Western Reserve J Int Law 36:375–419
2. Weinberg L, Pedahzur A, Hirsch-Hoefler S (2004) The challenges of conceptualizing terrorism. Terrorism Political Violence 16(4):777–794

3. Turk A (2008) Sociology of terrorism. In: Matson R (ed) The spirit of sociology: a reader. Pearson, Boston, pp 490–502
4. Hall S, Critcher C, Jefferson T, Clarke J, Roberts B (1978) Policing the crisis. Macmillan, London
5. Sederberg PC (1989) Terrorist myths: Illusion, rhetoric, and reality. Prentice-Hall, Englewood Cliffs
6. Zulaika J, Douglass W (1996) Terror and taboo: the follies fables, and faces of terrorism. Routledge, New York
7. Herman E, O'Sullivan G (1989) The terrorism industry: the experts and institutions that shape our view of terror. Pantheon Books, New York
8. Ganor B (2002) Defining terrorism: is one man's terrorist another man's freedom fighter? Police Pract 3(4):287–304
9. Coady T, O'Keefe M (eds) (2002) Terrorism and justice: moral argument in a threatened world. Melbourne University Press, Melbourne
10. George A (ed) (1991) Western state terrorism. Polity, Cambridge
11. Rummel RJ (1994) Death by government: genocide and mass murder in the twentieth century. Transaction, Rutgers
12. Wilkinson P (2003) Why modern terrorism? Differentiating types and distinguishing ideological motivations. In: Kegley CW Jr (ed) The new global terrorism: characteristics, causes, controls. Prentice Hall, Upper Saddle River, pp 106–138
13. de Swaan A (2004) Moord en de staat. Bert Bakker, Amsterdam
14. LaFree G, Dugan L (2007) Introducing the global terrorism database. Terrorism Political Violence 19:181–204
15. Seymour G (1975) Harry's game. Random House, New York
16. Sluka J (2002) What anthropologists should know about the concept of terrorism. Anthropology Today 18(2):22–23
17. Burton F, Stewart S (2008) The 'lone wolf' disconnect. STRATFOR global intelligence. http://www.stratfor.com/weekly/lone_wolf_disconnect. Accessed 3 Aug 2009
18. Vasilenko VI (2004) The concept and typology of terrorism. Statutes Decis 40(5):46–56
19. Spaaij R (2010) The enigma of lone wolf terrorism: an assessment. Stud Conflict Terrorism 33(9):854–870
20. Hoffman B (1998) Inside terrorism. Columbia University Press, New York
21. Hoffman B (2003) Al qaeda, trends in terrorism, and future potentialities: an assessment. RAND, Santa Monica
22. Mech LD, Boitani L (eds) (2003) Wolves: behavior, ecology, conservation. University of Chicago Press, Chicago
23. Fijnaut C (2011) Breivik was geen 'lone wolf'. BNR nieuwsradio, 30 Aug
24. Groth AN (1979) Men who rape: the psychology of the offender. Basic Books, New York
25. Dixon AL, Gassenheimer JB, Feldman Barr T (2003) Identifying the lone wolf: a team perspective. J Pers Selling Sales Manage 23(3):205–219
26. Feldman Barr T, Dixon AL, Gassenheimer JB (2005) Exploring the lone wolf phenomenon in student teams. J Marketing Edu 27(1):81–90
27. Pantucci R (2011) A typology of lone wolves: preliminary analysis of lone Islamist terrorists. ICSR, London
28. Kirby A (2007) The London bombers as 'self-starters': a case study in indigenous radicalisation and the emergence of autonomous cliques. Stud Conflict Terrorism 30(5): 415–428
29. Kushner H (2003) Encyclopedia of terrorism. Sage, Thousand Oaks
30. Juergensmeyer M (2000) Terror in the mind of God: the global rise of religious violence. University of California Press, Berkeley
31. Springer N (2009) Patterns of radicalization: identifying the markers and warning signs of domestic lone wolf terrorists in our midst. Unpublished master's thesis. Naval Postgraduate School, Monterey, CA

32. Hamm MS (2001) In bad company: america's terrorist underground. Northeastern University Press, Boston
33. Jenkins P (2003) Images of terror: what we can and can't know about terrorism. Aldine de Gruyter, New York
34. Breivik A (2011) 2083: a European declaration of independence. http://www.washingtonpost.com/r/2010-2019/WashingtonPost/2011/07/24/National-Politics/Graphics/2083+-+A+European+Declaration+of+Independence.pdf. Accessed 26 July 2011
35. BBC (2011) Norway: anders behring breivik claims 'two more cells'. BBC news, 25 July. http://www.bbc.co.uk/news/world-europe-14280210. Accessed 26 July 2011
36. Millar L (2011) I didn't act alone, norway attacker tells court. ABC news, 26 July. http://www.abc.net.au/news/2011-07-25/norway-attacks-suspect-arrives-in-court/2809930. Accessed 27 July 2011
37. Stewart S (2011) Norway: lessons from a successful lone wolf attacker. STRATFOR global intelligence. http://www.stratfor.com/weekly/20110727-norway-lessons-successful-lone-wolf-attacker. Accessed 30 July 2011
38. Stewart S (2011) Al qaeda's new video: a message of defeat. STRATFOR global intelligence. http://www.stratfor.com/weekly/20110608-AlQaedas-new-video-message-defeat. Accessed 30 July 2011
39. Kaczynski T (1995) Industrial society and its future (Unabomber's Manifesto). http://www.provokateur.com/webres/Unabomber%20Manifesto%20by%20Theodore%20Kaczynski. Accessed 8 June 2007
40. Englund W (2011) In diary, norwegian 'crusader' details months of preparation for attacks. The Washington Post, 25 July
41. Schwarz M (1999) Lebenslange Haft für österreichischen Bombenbauer. Berliner Zeitung, 11 Mar
42. Müller T (2006) Beestmensen: vermomming leugens en strategie van seriemoordenaars. Mets Schilt, Amsterdam
43. BBC (2000) Profile: copeland the killer. BBC News, 30 June
44. Buncombe A (2000) A man sexually confused and obsessed with the far right. The Independent, 30 June
45. Ames P (2011) Is anders behring breivik part of a movement? Global Post, 25 July. http://www.globalpost.com/dispatch/news/regions/europe/110724/europe-right-wing-political-parties-Breivik-manifesto. Accessed 26 Aug 2011
46. Laqueur W (1999) The new terrorism: fanaticism and the arms of mass destruction. Oxford University Press, Oxford
47. Jackson P (2011) Solo actor terrorism and the mythology of the lone wolf. In: Gable G, Jackson P (eds) Lone wolves: myth or reality?. Searchlight, Ilford, pp 79–88
48. Dishman C (2001) Terrorism, crime, and transformation. Stud Conflict Terrorism 24(1):43–58
49. Crenshaw M (2003) The causes of terrorism. in the new global terrorism: characteristics
50. Crelinsten RD (2009) Counterterrorism. Polity, Cambridge
51. Turchie T, Puckett K (2007) Hunting the American terrorist: the FBI's war on homegrown terror. History Publishing Company, Palisades
52. Quillen C (2002) A historical analysis of mass casualty bombers. Stud Conflict Terrorism 25(5):279–292
53. Stern J (2003) Terror in the name of God: why religious militants kill. HarperCollins, New York
54. Shane S, Johnston D (2009) Questions, not alarms, met exchanges with cleric. The New York Times, 11 Nov
55. Robbins L, Shane S (2009) Suspect in Ft. Hood shootings to remain in hospital. The New York Times, 22 Nov

Chapter 4
Incidence and Evolution

4.1 Lone Wolf Terrorism in Its Historical Context

Lone wolf terrorism is not a new phenomenon. Acts of terrorism carried out by single individuals can be found, for instance, in nineteenth century anarchism, with some proponents considering individual acts of violence to be an important part of revolutionary activity [1, 2].[5] Some leading Russian, Italian, French and German anarchist thinkers advocated a strategy of "propaganda by deed", urging individuals and small groups to kill those who represented an existing social order [2, 4, 5], For example, the Russian anarchist theorist Mikhail Bakunin (1814–1876) argued that since creating a vast and hierarchical organization would inevitably come to involve the use of coercive power, the anarchist revolutionary should preferably act individually or form small groups of like-minded individuals acting on their own initiative. Bakunin strongly believed in direct action and in the effectiveness of the example of a revolutionary few to spark off the spontaneous revolt of the masses [6]. Indeed, the notion of "propaganda by deed" inspired individual terrorist attacks in large parts of nineteenth century Europe, directed principally against institutions that were seen to represent the values of bourgeois society [2, 7]. In the twentieth century, however, anarchists ceased, in both theory and practice, to view individual terrorism as an important and rewarding strategy [1, 8].

Clearly lone wolf terrorism continued into the twentieth century, but its main political/ideological and geographical locations appeared to shift. Between 1940 and 1957, George Metesky, also known as the "Mad Bomber", planted 33 improvised explosive devices in New York, 22 of which exploded. Metesky hid his pipe bombs in public locations such as public restrooms, phone booths and theater seats. His bombs caused no fatalities, but 15 people sustained injuries.

[5] There is, however, no necessary association between anarchism and terrorism since many anarchists reject violence of any form. The association between the two seems to owe principally to a series of historical events in Russia and Eastern Europe rather than to some necessary feature of anarchist philosophy [1, 3].

R. Spaaij, *Understanding Lone Wolf Terrorism*, SpringerBriefs in Criminology,
DOI: 10.1007/978-94-007-2981-0_4,

Metesky placed his first explosive device outside a building of utility giant Consolidated Edison, on 16 November 1940. A former employee of the company, Metesky had suffered an on-site accident at the plant where he worked, and attributed his developing tuberculosis to that accident. When his disability claim was denied, Metesky wrote several angry letters to the company. Although his anger was principally directed at his former employer, over the years his ability to elude the police and the increasing sophistication and force of the bombings engendered anxiety in New Yorkers and humiliated the New York Police Department [9]. Following the publication of an open letter in the *New York Journal-American* that promised good treatment to the bomber if he would reveal himself, however, Metesky became involved in a public dialogue with the newspaper by responding with letters of his own. Details from these letters subsequently helped to bring about Metesky's arrest in 1957 [9].

In 1963, another high-profile lone wolf attack took place in the United States within the context of tense race relations. White supremacist Byron De La Beckwith shot and killed Medgar Evers, a 37-year-old field secretary for the National Association for the Advancement of Colored People (NAACP) in Jackson, Mississippi (e.g. [10]). In 1973 De La Beckwith was arrested in Lousiana with a bomb in his car, reportedly intent on murdering the regional director of the Anti-Defamation League (see Appendix). Although in both cases De La Beckwith acted on his own, it seems that he later joined the Ku Klux Klan. In 1994, 30 years after the murder, he was convicted to life in prison for the killing of Evers [11]. In an interview shortly before his arrest in 1990, De La Beckwith said that he was "willing to kill the evil in this country that would try to push me out" [12].

In the second half of the twentieth century lone wolf terrorism was particularly associated with White supremacists and antigovernment extremists in the United States, and especially with the "leaderless resistance" concept [13–16]. Leaderless resistance can be defined as "a kind of lone wolf operation in which an individual, or a very small, highly cohesive group, engages in acts of anti-state violence independent of any movement, leader, or network of support" [13, p. 80]. Kaplan traces the leaderless resistance concept back to the early 1970s, when Joseph Tommasi, co-founder of the National Socialist Liberation Front (NSLF), encouraged White supremacists to act resolutely and alone against the state. This commitment to act alone was in contrast to the relatively rigid, centralized command structure of many then-contemporary terrorist groups which were deemed vulnerable to detection, infiltration and prosecution by the state. The leaderless resistance concept was popularized by White supremacist Louis Beam, a Klansman with ties to Aryan Nations [17]. Beam published an essay advocating leaderless resistance as a strategy to counteract the destruction of right-wing militias by US law enforcement agencies. Beam [18] writes: "Let the coming night be filled with a 1,000 points of resistance. Like the fog which forms when conditions are right and disappears when they are not, so must the resistance to tyranny be". His vision is one where "all individuals and groups operate independently of each other, and never report to a central headquarters or single leader for direction or instruction". Beam goes on to assert: "It is the duty of every patriot to make the tyrant's life miserable. When one fails to do so he not only fails himself, but his people". This mindset shifts both agency and accountability from the group to the individual or autonomous collective [19]. Beam credits the leaderless resistance concept to Colonel Ulius Louis Amoss, who in the early 1960s proposed the strategy as a defence against a Communist takeover of the United States.

In the late 1990s, the influential White supremacists Tom Metzger and Alex Curtis used the term "lone wolf" within the context of their specific, political agenda [20]. They envisioned lone wolf and small cell attacks to be considerably more difficult to detect than conventional terrorism, and encouraged like-minded individuals to conduct such attacks on their own as part of a wider narrative of revolutionary action emerging from radicalized sectors of America's far right [16]. These actions were seen by White supremacists as a legitimate means to overthrow an allegedly corrupt political system and replace it with their new order. Metzger's [51] *Laws for the Lone Wolf*, for example, provides the following encouragement to would-be lone wolves:

> Anyone is capable of being a Lone Wolf. Resistance is a lifestyle, each performs to his or her individual abilities. Success and experience will come in time. ... Never rush into anything, time and planning are keys to success. Never attempt anything beyond your own abilities, failure could lead to disaster. ... Never truly admit to anything. ... Others will notice your activities, but never try to take any credit for them, your success should be all the recognition you need. ... Exist and fight as lone wolves or in a small cell and you will last longer and be at peak performance. ... Remember, those who have come before you are counting on you, those who will come after you are depending on you. Think White, act White, be White!

Media use of the term "lone wolf" has subsequently helped to popularize the concept, especially within journalist, academic and practitioner settings [16].

Both Metzger and Curtis recognized the opportunities the Internet affords for the dissemination of information and the communication with fellow militants. The recent attacks in Norway resonate with their ideas and illustrate how the Internet has become a convenient medium for the dissemination and communication of radical material. While the accused perpetrator Anders Breivik does not express any anti-Semitism in his manifesto and is arguably closer to counterjihad thought [21], his anti-immigration and anti-Marxist ideology has been influenced by the far right and his modus operandi shows important parallels with the leaderless resistance concept, as discussed at length in Chaps. 6 and 7.

Leaderless resistance of course has been advocated and used by a variety of militant actors, including Christian fundamentalists, jihadists, militant anarchists, animal rights and radical environmental activists [22–24], albeit to varying degrees. Leaderless resistance should therefore not be thought of as merely a strategy of the radical right, even if it developed from within this particular context. For example, in *A Declaration of War: Killing People to Save Animals and the Environment* (1991) radical animal rights activist "Screaming Wolf" describes the strategy of militant interventionism as a necessary measure for animal liberation and urges "liberators" to work alone or with one or two other tried and true friends. Screaming Wolf [25, p. 55] asserts:

> [L]iberators have no leader. We are not organized in the traditional sense of the word. We are independent people accepting the responsibility of freeing our family members from human oppression. We don't take responsibility for one another's actions. We are empowered to do our own actions in accordance with our own conscience.

In recent times Al Qaeda and related radical Islamist groups have encouraged lone wolf attacks as an effective strategy to strike against the enemy—loosely referred to as "the West", "Crusaders", or "Zionists"—in videos and online magazines. The ideas of Abu Mus'ab al-Suri, and in particular his book *The Global Islamic Resistance Call*, feature in many of these messages. The English-language online magazine *Inspire* published by Al Qaeda in the Arabian Peninsula (AQAP), has reprinted several parts of this book in which al-Suri outlines strategies for future jihadists, with an emphasis on unorganized cells and leaderless jihad. The issue of "individual terrorism jihad" (*jihad al-irhab al-fardi*), that is, secret jihadi operations performed by a single individual or small units totally separated from each other, is one of al-Suri's main principles [26]. In the tactical implementation of this strategy, some radicalized Muslims across the world undertake local unconnected attacks against western interests, gradually "transforming the phenomenon of random and opportunistic violence into what appears to be a mass movement with coordination and direction" [27, p. 6]. The purpose of individual jihad then is, *inter alia*, to confuse and overburden hostile intelligence and security services, and it is seen to have distinct tactical advantages [28].

Al Qaeda's latest attempt to encourage Islamist militants to undertake lone wolf operations in the West is the video "You Are Responsible Only for Yourself". The video, released on 2 June 2011 by Al Qaeda's media arm As-Sahab, urges Islamist militants in the West to take up arms and target major institutions and public figures. The core message: "Do not rely on others, take the task upon yourself" [29]. The video asserts that it is easy and effective to strike the enemy in their home countries. The American Al Qaeda operative Adam Gadahn states in the video: "Muslims in the West have to remember that they are perfectly placed to play an important and decisive part in the jihad against the Zionists and Crusaders". The video statement also calls on militants to develop the Internet skills to attack the West in cyberspace [30]. On another occasion, Gadahn openly praised Nidal Hassan Malik—the man who killed 13 people at Fort Hood in 2009—and called upon other Muslims to follow his lead [31].

It has been argued that in large part as a consequence of the extensive counterterrorism efforts since 9/11, lone wolf attacks are in fact Al Qaeda's "favorite new strategy", at least in the United States [32]. The Danish Centre for Terror Analysis [33, p. 5] concludes that Al Qaeda "seems to supplement its traditional focus on complex operations with [a] focus on individual attacks … [in] an attempt to make the organisation more to the point and effective after having for a long period of time had limited possibilities for central planning as a result of the international efforts against terrorism". However, Stewart [34] interprets this relative shift in focus, and the very call to leaderless resistance, as "an admission of defeat" and an indication that, in practice, Al Qaeda and its franchise groups may have been "rendered transnationally impotent".

4.2 Incidence and Lethality

How common, then, are solo-actor terrorist attacks of the kind described above, and how deadly are they? The database of lone wolf terrorism enables us to provide empirically grounded answers to these questions. The data indicate that in the 15 countries under study, there were a total of 88 identified lone wolves during the period 1968–2010, and that these lone wolves carried out a total of (at least) 198 attacks. This means that lone wolf terrorist attacks account for roughly 1.8% of all terrorist incidents from 1968 to 2010 in these 15 countries (198 of a total of 11,235 terrorist incidents, as recorded in the Global Terrorism Database). This finding suggests that, statistically speaking, lone wolf terrorism is a relatively marginal phenomenon, with the rare occurrence of lone wolf terrorist attacks (at an average rate of 4.7 per year across all 15 countries) making them difficult to categorize and pattern, let alone predict [35]. It should be reiterated, however, that this figure is a conservative estimate. As discussed in Chap. 2, ambiguous incidents were excluded from the database (see Appendix) as much as possible, for example those incidents where the perpetrator was unknown or a political motive appeared to be absent. There is also likely to be a "hidden figure" of lone wolf terrorism (and terrorism in general) unreported to/by the authorities or news media and unregistered in the Global Terrorism Database and RAND-MIPT Terrorism Knowledge Base (see Chap. 2).

Looking at these figures, one could ask: why have there not been *more* lone wolf terrorist attacks? This question is particularly relevant considering the popularity of the leaderless resistance strategy among extremist groups from a variety of political, ideological and religious backgrounds. One main reason is that, as discussed in Chap. 6, very few individuals radicalize to the point where they see themselves as bearers of the responsibility for violent actions, due in part to the associated consequences (e.g. imprisonment, death). A second reason is that it can be difficult to translate theory into action; that is, there is often a disconnect between intention and capability [36]. Collins [52] offers an intriguing sociological explanation as to why this may be so. For Collins, performing an act of violence is difficult because it goes against the grain of normal interaction rituals. No matter how ideologically committed would-be terrorists are, and how strong their support network, they can only be successful if they overcome confrontational tension and fear. Terrorists, Collins argues, use confrontation-minimizing tactics in an attempt to circumvent the barrier of confrontational tension that all violence must surmount. These tactics are "virtually always carried out by small groups acting in concert, not only because they need the manpower, but also because they use group emotional solidarity to overcome confrontational tension" [52]. Overcoming confrontational tension may be particularly challenging for a lone wolf terrorist who by definition lacks strong group emotional solidarity, even though, as noted in Chap. 3, they may imagine or seek such solidarity.

In his 1,517-page manifesto, the accused Norwegian lone wolf Anders Breivik describes in his own words the challenges of carrying out individual terrorism. His remarks that very few individuals are cut out for terrorist violence are of particular interest here. In the light of the above explanations, Breivik's [37, p. 831] comments appear to be more than mere self-aggrandizement:

> He must have a strong conviction, be self-confident, be highly motivated, hard working and with the practical knowledge required in order to successfully execute an operation alone (logistics, finance and execution). Furthermore, he must be willing to martyr himself in the final operation. ... A Cell commander is a volunteer and will often be working alone. Therefore the traditional military "sheep mentality" is only a liability. It's imperative that the individual is creative, resourceful, ideologically self-confident and has the ability to maintain high moral. This is the reason why very few individuals are cut out for activity (perhaps only 1 out of 1,000 conservative activists).

The relevance of these issues to the mindset and modus operandi of lone wolf terrorists will be further explored in the next chapters.

Considering the abovementioned disconnect between intention and capability, it is perhaps unsurprising that most lone wolf terrorist attacks claim relatively few lives. It has been argued that lone wolves are likely to have little impact on society when compared to vast terrorist organizations due in large part to their comparatively limited resources and capabilities [38, 39]. On the other hand, some analysts point out that lone wolf terrorists "can be exceptionally dangerous" and that "if such lone terrorists have access to high technologies, their acts may be very destructive" [40, p. 54]. The 22 July 2011 attacks in Norway which claimed a total of 77 lives are cases in point. Moreover, as noted earlier, lone wolf terrorists may be more difficult to detect and pose specific counterterrorism challenges. It should be kept in mind, however, that the number of casualties from attacks is not necessarily a good indicator of the impact of lone wolf terrorism. After all, as argued in Chap. 3, from the terrorist's perspective the immediate target is usually of secondary import to the broader audience in which he or she seeks to install fear. The mantra of the terrorist typically is "kill one, frighten 10,000", a phrase often attributed to Chinese war theorist Sun Tzu. In the modern information age [41], the axiom might even be: "Kill one, frighten 10 million".

What do the cross-national data tell us about the lethality of lone wolf terrorism? In total, the 198 lone wolf attacks in the research sample claimed at least 123 lives (including in some instances the lives of the perpetrators themselves) and injured hundreds more. Put differently, lone wolf terrorism averages 0.62 deaths per incident. This rate is low compared to that for all terrorist attacks in the 15 countries under study, which average roughly 1.6 deaths per attack (as recorded in the Global Terrorism Database). Moreover, there is no evidence that the overall lethality of lone wolf terrorism is on the increase. This is an interesting finding when compared to the growing lethality of terrorism in general [42], and raises the important question of why lone wolf terrorism is, on average, significantly less lethal than group-actor terrorism. Major reasons for this are that lone wolves lack organizational size, do not normally maintain extensive alliance connections with peers, and do not have control over territory, all of which are important predictors

Table 4.1 Top five most lethal lone wolves

Name	Location	Year(s)	Fatalities
Joseph Paul Franklin	United States	1976–1980	18
Nidal Malik Hassan	United States	2009	13
Mark Essex	United States	1972–1973	10
Neal Long	United States	1972–1975	7
Colin Ferguson	United States	1993	6

American White supremacist Joseph Christopher, also known as the ".22-Caliber Killer", estimated that his murder spree in 1980 had cost at least 13 lives [44]; however the GTD and TKB combined attribute only five murders to Christopher, who was sentenced to 60 years in prison.

of lethality [43]. A closely related reason is the disconnect that often exists between intention and capability, as discussed at length in Chap. 7.

The average fatality rate conceals the significant variations in the number of fatalities caused by lone wolf terrorist attacks. Table 4.1 lists the five lone wolves in the research sample whose actions caused the most casualties. No lone wolf terrorist within the sample claimed more than 18 lives as a result of their actions, whether their terrorism consisted of a single attack or a series of attacks (between 2 and 30). Black militant Colin Ferguson and Islamist Nidal Malik Hassan are the only lone wolves in Table 4.1 who carried out just one attack. All five perpetrators listed in Table 4.1 were US citizens and carried out their attacks in the United States; three of them did so more than 3 decades ago. At the other end of the spectrum, several lone wolf attacks failed to claim any lives or only the life of the perpetrator. This is also a common occurrence in group-actor terrorism; approximately three-quarters of all terrorist attacks in the 15 countries did not cause any casualties (as recorded in the Global Terrorism Database).

While lone wolf terrorist attacks typically claim only a small number of lives, the above data demonstrate that the recent attacks in Norway are exceptional in terms of their death toll of 77. The 1995 Oklahoma City bombing is frequently mentioned in this context because of its lethality; however, as I have argued in Chap. 3, this attack does not, strictly speaking, qualify as lone wolf terrorism because Timothy McVeigh's accomplice, Terry Nichols, played a considerable role in the preparations for the attack. It can be argued that Nichols' support helped McVeigh translate theory into action, for example in helping to select the target (the Alfred P. Murray Federal Building), purchase components for the bomb, and so forth [45, 46].

4.3 Lone Wolf Terrorism Across Space and Time

The previous section presented some general patterns regarding the incidence and lethality of lone wolf terrorism. Beyond these generalities, however, there are important cross-national variations which require a closer look. Figure 4.1 shows

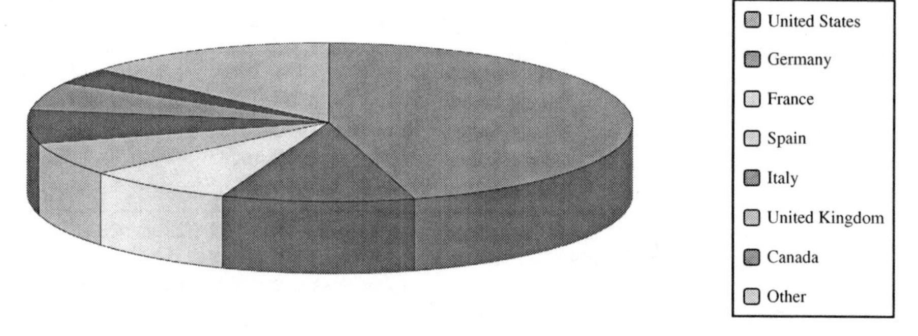

Fig. 4.1 Geographical distribution of lone wolf terrorists

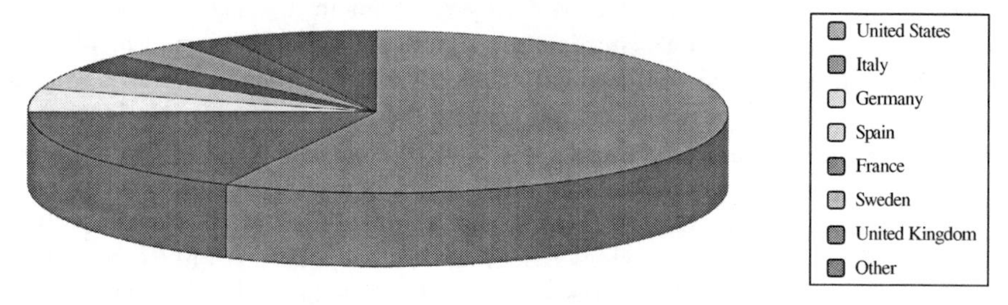

Fig. 4.2 Geographical distribution of lone wolf terrorist attacks

that lone wolf terrorism is unevenly distributed across the 15 countries. It is significantly more prevalent in the United States than in the other countries, with the US cases (40 in total) accounting for 45% of all cases (n = 88). Outside of the United States, the countries with the highest number of lone wolves during the period 1968–2010 are Germany (nine), France (seven), Spain (six), Italy (six) and the United Kingdom (five).

If we look at the total number of attacks carried out by these lone wolves (n = 198), the picture is slightly different, as shown in Fig. 4.2. The 113 recorded lone wolf terrorist attacks in the United States make up 57% of all terrorist attacks committed by lone individuals in the 15 countries, followed by Italy which experienced 35 lone wolf terrorist attacks between 1968 and 2010, amounting to 18% of the total. Many of the attacks in the United States and Italy can be attributed to a small number of individuals, most notably the "Italian Unabomber" (30 attacks), Luke Helder (18 attacks), Theodore Kaczynski (16 attacks), Joseph Paul Franklin (16 attacks) and Rachelle Shannon (9 attacks). In conjunction, these five individuals are believed to be responsible for 89 attacks, which constitute approximately 45% of all lone wolf terrorist attacks in the 15 countries between 1968 and 2010.

The data on the geographical distribution of lone wolf terrorism highlight the comparatively high incidence of lone wolf terrorism in the United States. In that

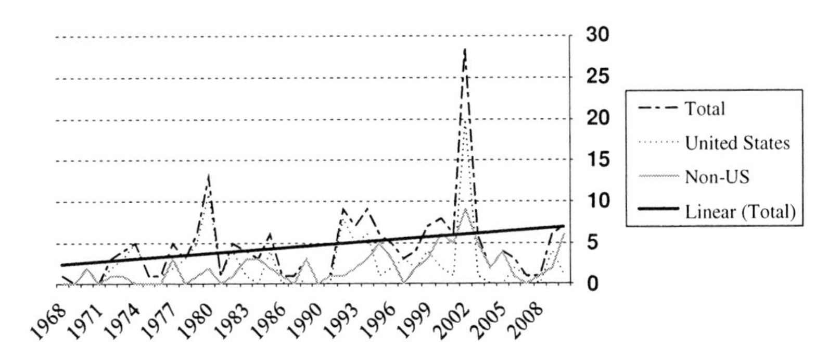

Fig. 4.3 Lone wolf terrorism over time, 1968–2010

country, lone wolf terrorist attacks account for 5% of all terrorist attacks between 1968 and 2010 (2,235 incidents, as recorded in the Global Terrorism Database), a percentage that is significantly higher than in the other countries in the research sample (as noted, 1.8% of all terrorist incidents were carried out by lone wolves). This finding verifies Hewitt's [47] conclusion that lone wolf terrorism is predominantly, though clearly not exclusively, a US phenomenon. "American terrorism", Hewitt [47, p. 78] argues, "differs from terrorism in other countries in that a significant proportion of terrorist attacks have been carried out by unaffiliated individuals rather than by members of terrorist organizations". The comparatively high incidence of lone wolf terrorism in the United States can be partly explained by the popularity of the leaderless resistance concept among right-wing extremists and anti-abortion activists in that country [48]. Furthermore, lone wolf terrorism may be seen in part as the remnants of successfully combated and disrupted group-actor terrorism in the United States (Hewitt, in [49]). Indeed, the concept of leaderless resistance, as articulated by White supremacist Louis Beam and others, largely developed as a reponse to the disruption and round-up of violent extremist networks by US law enforcement agencies. Louis Beam [18] himself describes leaderless resistance as "a child of necessity", because "the alternatives to it have been shown to be unworkable or impractical". As noted earlier, more recently other extremist movements have also come to view leaderless resistance as having distinct tactical advantages over group-actor terrorism.

Hewitt [47, p. 79] concludes that lone wolf terrorism in the United States "has greatly increased in recent decades". During the period 1955–1977, 7% of all victims of terrorism in the United States were reportedly killed by unaffiliated individuals, but between 1978 and 1999 this rose to 26% [47, p. 78]. However, Hewitt's analysis also includes attacks by couples and trios (which account for approximately one-quarter of cases, including the Oklahoma City bombing which killed 168 people), since he considers a terrorist group to consist of at least four individuals. Hewitt's findings seem to support the view of US authorities that lone wolf terrorism in the United States is an ascending threat (see Chap. 1).

The cross-national data can shed further light on the development of lone wolf terrorism over time. Figure 4.3 shows the number of lone wolf terrorist attacks

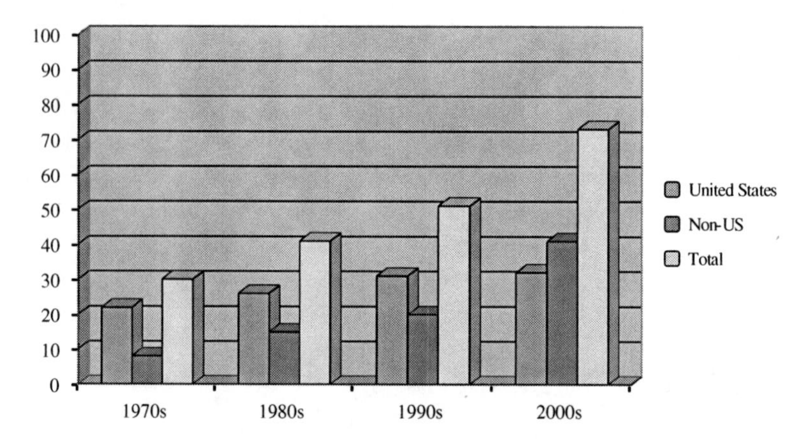

Fig. 4.4 Four decades of lone wolf terrorism, 1970s–2000s

(n = 198) over a 42 year period, mapping the United States, non-United States and total attacks in the database as well as a linear trendline. Overall, there has been a slight rise in the number of lone wolf terrorist attacks over time, yet a year-by-year visualization of lone wolf terrorism does not reveal a clear, single trend. What Fig. 4.3 does show, however, is that during the period 1968–2010 there were three significant spikes in lone wolf terrorist activity: first, in the early 1980s, predominantly in the United States (i.e. Joseph Paul Franklin, Joseph Christopher and Theodore Kaczynski); second, in the early-to-mid 1990s, mainly in the United States and to a lesser degree in Europe; and, third, in the early 2000s, particularly in the United States, Italy and Spain.

In order to identify possible trends in the extent of lone wolf terrorism over a prolonged period of time, it is useful to establish a more aggregate picture that captures changes across decades. Figure 4.4 compares the incidence of lone wolf terrorist attacks (n = 198) across 4 decades, showing a gradual increase in the number of lone wolf terrorist attacks both within the United States and, more rapidly, outside the United States. Between the 1970s and 2000s, the total number of lone wolf terrorist attacks per decade rose by 45% (from 22 to 32) in the United States and by a massive 412% (from 8 to 41) in the other 14 countries combined. In the 2000s, the combined total of non-US lone wolf terrorist attacks exceeded the total number of attacks within the United States for the first time. However, as noted earlier, there exist significant variations in the incidence of lone wolf terrorism across these 14 countries, ranging from a total of 35 attacks in Italy to zero in the Czech Republic. Overall, the total number of lone wolf attacks has grown from 30 in the 1970s to 73 in the 2000s, an increase of 143%.

These findings support Hewitt's [47] conclusion that in the United States lone wolf terrorism has increased in recent decades, but they also show that this increase is not as great as Hewitt suggests, at least not in terms of the *number* of attacks. In fact, the most marked increase in lone wolf terrorism in recent decades can be found in Europe, where the number of attacks quadrupled between the

1970s and 2000s.[6] In the next chapters these findings will be further explored in relation to other key dimensions of lone wolf terrorism. Specifically, Chap. 5 examines the ideologies and motivational patterns that give rise to lone wolf terrorism.

References

1. Novak D (1954) Anarchism and individual terrorism. Can J Econ Political Sci 20(2):176–184
2. Woodcock G (2004) Anarchism: a history of libertarian ideas and movements. Broadview Press, Peterborough 1986
3. Taylor M (1988) The terrorist. Brassey's Defence Publishers, London
4. Fleming M (1979) The anarchist way to socialism. Rowman and Littlefield, Totowa
5. Garrison A (2004) Defining terrorism: philosophy of the bomb, propaganda by deed and change through fear and violence. Crim Justice Stud 17(3):259–279
6. Joll J (1970) Anarchism: a living tradition. Gov Oppos 5(4):541–554
7. Kushner H (2003) Encyclopedia of terrorism. Sage, Thousand Oaks
8. Laqueur W (1977) Terrorism. Weidenfeld & Nicholson, London
9. Greenburg M (2011) The mad bomber of New York: the extraordinary true story of the manhunt that paralyzed a city. Union Square Press, New York
10. Vollers M (1995) Ghosts of mississippi: the murder of Medgar Evers, the trials of Byron De La Beckwith, and the haunting of the new south. Back Bay Books, Boston
11. Stout D (2001) Byron De La Beckwith dies; killer of Medgar Evers was 80. The New York Times, 23 January
12. Associated Press (2001) Byron De La Beckwith; white supremacist served life for '63 killing of Medgar Evers. Los Angeles Times, 24 January
13. Kaplan J (1997) Leaderless resistance. Terrorism Political Violence 9(3):80–95
14. Thomas J (1999) New face of terror crimes: 'lone wolf' weaned on hate. The New York Times, 1, 16 August
15. Martin G (2003) Understanding terrorism: challenges, perspectives, and issues. Sage, Thousands Oaks
16. Jackson P (2011) Solo actor terrorism and the mythology of the lone wolf. In: Gable G, Jackson P (eds) Lone wolves: myth or reality?. Searchlight, Ilford, pp 79–88
17. Hamilton NA (1996) Militias in America: a reference handbook. ABC-CLIO, Santa Barbara
18. Beam L (1992) Leaderless resistance. Seditionist 12. http://www.louisbeam.com/leaderless.htm. Accessed 2 June 2007
19. Borum R (2011) Lone wolf terrorism. In: Martin CG (ed) The SAGE encyclopedia of terrorism, 2nd edn. Sage, London, pp 361–362
20. Anti-defamation league (2002) Extremism in America. http://www.adl.org/learn/ext_us/curtis.asp?LEARN_Cat=Extremism&LEARN_SubCat=Extremism_in_America&xpicked=2&item=curtis. Accessed 1 June 2007

---

[6] This conclusion differs from my earlier assessment of lone wolf terrorism in these countries, which found that there had been no comparable increase in lone wolf terrorism in the European countries under study [48, 50]. This discrepancy has been minimized by the subsequent revision and expansion of the lone wolf terrorism database (see Appendix) using the GTD and other open-source material, which has enabled me to resolve most of the gaps and inconsistencies in the data. The present findings should be considered significantly more reliable and conclusive because they draw on a more complete and accurate data set. Furthermore, the findings presented here show the total number of *attacks*, whereas my previous publications mainly show the number of *individuals* carrying out lone wolf attacks in any given year or decade.

21. Hegghammer T (2011) The rise of the macro-nationalists. The New York Times, 30 July, SR5. http://www.nytimes.com/2011/07/31/opinion/sunday/the-rise-of-the-macro-nationalists.html. Accessed 3 Aug 2011
22. Joosse P (2007) Leaderless resistance and ideological inclusion: the case of the earth liberation front. Terrorism Political Violence 19(3):351–368
23. Sageman M (2008) Leaderless jihad: terror networks in the twenty first century. University of Pennsylvania Press, Philadelphia
24. Stewart S (2011) Norway: lessons from a successful lone wolf attacker. STRATFOR global intelligence. http://www.stratfor.com/weekly/20110727-norway-lessons-successful-lone-wolf-attacker. Accessed 30 July 2011
25. Wolf S (1991) A declaration of war: killing people to save animals and the environment. Reach Out Publications, Salt Lake City, UT. http://www.reachoutpub.com/dow_p.pdf. Accessed 4 July 2007
26. Lia B (2008) Architect of global jihad: the life of Al Qaeda strategist Abu Mus'ab al-Suri. Columbia University Press, New York
27. Zabel SE (2007) The military strategy of global jihad. Strategic Studies Institute, Washington
28. Batal al-Shishani M (2011) Al qaeda leader targets 'near enemy'. Asia Times Online, 17 June. http://www.atimes.com/atimes/South_Asia/MF17Df01.html. Accessed 16 Aug 2011
29. MEMRI (2011) In new Al Qaeda Al-Sahab video, American Al Qaeda operative Adam Gadahn gives tips on how to attack American targets and world leaders. Middle East Media Research Institute Report 3886, 3 June. http://www.memri.org/report/en/0/0/0/0/0/0/5340.htm
30. Maclean W (2011) After bin Laden, militants flood net with threats. Reuters, 27 July. http://af.reuters.com/article/worldNews/idAFTRE75Q4G120110627?pageNumber=1&virtualBrandChannel=0. Accessed 18 Aug 2011
31. MEMRI (2010) Adam Gadahn praises Nidal Hasan, calls for more lone wolf attacks. Middle East Media Research Institute, 7 March. http://m.memri.org/14499/show/3e6218ed0bd0b4f076dcb8ede26e9799&t=35ca859c9504cb24dd041cd6a8784a1e
32. O'Connor T (2011) Lone wolf terrorism. http://www.drtomoconnor.com/3400/3400lect05a.htm. Accessed 29 July 2011
33. Centre for Terror Analysis (2011) The threat from solo terrorism and lone wolf terrorism. Danish Security and Intelligence Service, Copenhagen
34. Stewart S (2011) Al Qaeda's new video: a message of defeat. STRATFOR global intelligence. http://www.stratfor.com/weekly/20110608-AlQaedas-new-video-message-defeat. Accessed 30 July 2011
35. Bakker E, de Graaf B (2010) Lone wolves: how to prevent this phenomenon?. International Centre for Counter-Terrorism, The Hague
36. Stewart S, Burton F (2008) Lone wolf lessons. STRATFOR global intelligence. http://www.stratfor.com/weekly/20090603_lone_wolf_lessons. Accessed 4 Nov 2010
37. Breivik A (2011) 2083: a European declaration of independence. http://www.washingtonpost.com/r/2010-2019/WashingtonPost/2011/07/24/National-Politics/Graphics/2083+-+A+European+Declaration+of+Independence.pdf. Accessed 26 July 2011
38. Stern J (2003) Terror in the name of God: why religious militants kill. HarperCollins, New York
39. Schuster H, Stone C (2005) Hunting Eric Rudolph. Berkley Books, New York
40. Vasilenko VI (2004) The concept and typology of terrorism. Statutes Decis 40(5):46–56
41. Castells M (2010) The information age: economy, society and culture, vol 1–3, 2nd edn. Wiley-Blackwell, Oxford
42. Enders W, Sandler T (2005) After 9/11: Is it all different now? J Confl Resolut 49(2):259–277
43. Asal V, Rethemeyer RK (2008) The nature of the beast: organizational structures and the lethality of terrorist attacks. J Politics 70(2):437–449
44. Wilson C (2008) Serial killer investigations. Wakefield Press, Kent Town
45. Michel L, Herbeck D (2001) American terrorist. Timothy McVeigh and the Oklahoma City bombing. Regan Books, New York

46. Springer (2009) Patterns of radicalization: identifying the markers and warning signs of domestic lone wolf terrorists in our midst. Unpublished master's thesis. Naval Postgraduate School, Monterey
47. Hewitt C (2003) Understanding terrorism in America: from the Klan to al Qaeda. Routledge, New York
48. Spaaij R (2010) The enigma of lone wolf terrorism: an assessment. Stud Confl Terrorism 33(9):854–870
49. Bakker E, de Graaf B (2010) Expert meeting lone wolves: summary of proceedings. International Centre for Counter-Terrorism, The Hague
50. Spaaij R (2007) Lone-wolf terrorism. Report for the European Commission Sixth Framework program Transnational Terrorism, Security and the Rule of Law. COT Institute for Safety, Security and Crisis Management, The Hague
51. Metzger T (n.d.) Laws for the lone wolf. http://www.resist.com/Articles/literature/LawsForTheLoneWolfByTomMetzger.htm. Accessed 15 August 2011
52. Collins R (2008) Violence: a micro-sociological theory. Princeton University Press, Princeton

Chapter 5
Motivations and Ideologies

In the previous chapter it was argued that although historically the lone wolf strategy has been particularly advocated within radicalized sections of America's far right, it is not restricted to that milieu as lone wolf terrorists come from a variety of political, ideological and religious backgrounds. The database of lone wolf terrorism (see Appendix) provides further insight into the ideological sources of lone wolf terrorist attacks, and enables the identification of different categories of lone wolf terrorists based on their ideologies. Figure 5.1 indicates that among those identified, the main ideological sources of lone wolf terrorism in the 15 countries in the research sample are right-wing extremism/White supremacy (17%), Islamism (15%), anti-abortion (8%) and nationalism/separatism (7%), respectively.

The relative prevalence of right-wing extremism and White supremacy as ideological sources of lone wolf terrorism reflects the popularity of the lone wolf strategy within far right circles (in some cases, especially in the United States, extreme-right lone wolves also draw on Christian Identity beliefs). It is in this context that the US Department of Homeland Security [1, p. 7] states that White supremacist lone wolves currently pose the most significant domestic terrorist threat in the United States, referring to the "dangers of rightwing extremists embracing the tactics of 'leaderless resistance' and of lone wolves carrying out acts of violence". The Appendix highlights that in recent years a number of European lone wolves have also been inspired by extreme-right or White supremacist beliefs. Nonetheless, Fig. 5.1 clearly indicates that right-wing extremism and White supremacy are not the only ideologies that can underpin lone wolf terrorist attacks. Especially in recent years, the number of lone wolf terrorist attacks inspired by radical Islamism appears to have been on the rise, possibly partly in response to the call by Al Qaeda ideologues for individual jihad (see Chap. 4, [2]). In 2009 and 2010 alone, radical Islamism most likely inspired at least seven lone wolves to mount attacks: four in the United States, one in the United Kingdom, one in Italy and one in Sweden.

Significantly, in one-third of the incidents the perpetrator's ideological convictions remain unknown or unclear. One reason for this is the gaps in the

R. Spaaij, *Understanding Lone Wolf Terrorism*, SpringerBriefs in Criminology,
DOI: 10.1007/978-94-007-2981-0_5, © The Author(s) 2012

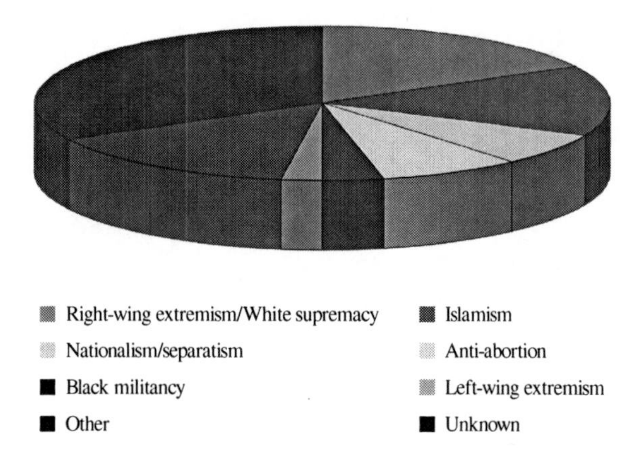

Fig. 5.1 Ideological sources of lone wolf terrorism

information contained in the GTD and TKB (and in the open sources upon which they draw) with regard to the motivations of lone wolf terrorists (see Chap. 2). A second reason is that some lone wolves may be secretive about their ideology in order not to incriminate themselves or fellow militants. For example, American White supremacist Tom Metzger [43], an influential advocate of the lone wolf strategy within far-right circles, argues: "No matter what the ideology many modern lone wolves most likely have been involved with, in most successful cases their ideology is kept secret, some even taking it to the grave". Elsewhere, Metzger [44] gives the following advice to would-be lone wolves:

> Never utter more than the 5 Words to any agent or representative of ZOG [Zionist Occupation Goverment]: "I Have Nothing To Say." There are no exceptions. Anyone who does talk must be shunned from the movement forever. Former associates of the talker may consider much harsher punishment. Never talk to a Grand Jury even when faced with contempt of court. No exceptions.

In a similar vein, Volkert van der Graaf, who in 2002 killed the Dutch politician Pim Fortuyn, wrote in a letter to his girlfriend prior to his trial: "Whenever I give a statement to the court or the media, I do not have to tell the truth necessarily. For the public at large the truth is not important, whereas it ought to be functional" [3]. On most occasions, van der Graaf has refused to comment on the reason behind his action. The district attorney who led van der Graaf's prosecution recognizes this issue, stating that "the whole truth is only inside the suspect's head, and in my view he has not given us full disclosure of events" [4]. Unsurprisingly, then, many questions surrounding van der Graaf's true motives remain unanswered [5, 6], not least with regard to the role of personal aversion and his presumed ideological affiliation with the radical fringe of the animal rights movement.

A third and arguably the most important reason why in several cases the exact motivation behind a lone wolf terrorist attack remains unclear, is that protagonists of lone wolf terrorism often combine the broad structures of a more prevalent extreme ideology with their own personal grievances. Thus, lone wolves tend to create their own individualized ideologies from a mixture of broader political, religious or social aims and personal frustrations and aversion [7, 8]. In this respect, the ideological sources identified in Fig. 5.1 are inevitably static and reductionistic; they show neither developmental processes (e.g. how a lone wolf's motivations evolve over time) nor ideological/motivational mixtures. Even in certain well-publicized cases, the perpetrators' motivations are far from straightforward and do not easily fit ideal types. I have included these cases in the 'unknown' category. Take for example the American lone wolf terrorist Eric Rudolph, who was sentenced to life in prison for four bombings between 1996 and 1998 that claimed three lives and wounded more than 120 others. In their comprehensive analysis of Eric Rudolph's terrorist campaign, Schuster and Stone [9, p. 356] ask:

> So who is the real Eric Rudolph? Did he bomb and kill in the name of Christian Identity, some religiously twisted version of white supremacy? Or had he genuinely been motivated by antiabortion fervor alone?... It could easily be a combination of both. Eric Rudolph may simply not know or at this point be able to distinguish why he said he bombed and killed from what he actually felt and intended at the time.

Maryanne Vollers [10], who explores in depth Rudolph's opposition to abortion (which she identifies as his avowed motive), his links to neo-Nazis and religious extremists, and his personal disaffection, draws a similar conclusion.

The Rudolph case illustrates the argument made in Chap. 3 that assigning a clear-cut motive or ideology to solo actor terrorists is often a problematic exercise. The 22 July 2011 attacks in Norway raise similar questions. Numerous news media, including the *Wall Street Journal* and *Washington Post*, initially attributed the attacks to jihadists. For example, shortly after the first attack it was stated in *Foreign Policy* that "the only concrete supposition that would emerge in a Norwegian context would be Al Qaeda" [11]. Subsequent evidence revealed, however, that the accused perpetrator was in fact an ethnic Norwegian man inspired by far-right beliefs, thus generating fierce debate regarding the threat of right-wing extremism in Norway and beyond. Notwithstanding extreme-right motives being attributed to the accused perpetrator, in several respects the Norwegian attacks are more complex than they might seem at first glance. This point is powerfully made by Hegghammer [12, SR5], who argues that whilst Breivik's manifesto appears to be "a fairly standard ideological treatise of the far right"—for example, it evokes several of the far right's central themes and cites numerous right-wing ideologues—on closer inspection Breivik's worldview "does not fit squarely into any of the established categories of right-wing ideology".

According to Hegghammer [12], much of Breivik's manifesto is inspired by a relatively new right-wing intellectual current referred to as counterjihad, which has gained substantial momentum since 9/11. However, by advocating mass violence and detailing how this could be planned and executed, Breivik goes much further than counterjihad ideologues have ever done, and several of the leading counterjihad ideologues have, in fact, strongly condemned Breivik's purported actions (see Chap. 6). Hegghammer [12, SR5] posits that the more belligerent part of Breivik's ideology has "less in common with counterjihad than with its archenemy", Al Qaeda. For example, both Breivik and Al Qaeda see themselves as engaged in a civilizational war between the West and Islam that extends back to the Crusades, and both fight on behalf of transnational entities: Europe and the ummah (a transnational community of Muslims; see [13]), respectively. These similarities, Hegghammer contends, suggest that Breivik and Al Qaeda are manifestations of the same generic ideological phenomenon: macro-nationalism—a variant of nationalism applied to clusters of nation-states held together by a notion of shared (transnational) identity. Extreme macro-nationalists, then, view their people as being under attack and fight in their defence.

That protagonists of lone wolf terrorism often combine the broad structures of a more prevalent extreme ideology with their own personal grievances and concerns is one of the key conclusions to be drawn from the qualitative case studies. All five cases demonstrate a variable, complex combination of political, ideological and personal motives. Let us first consider the case of Theodore Kaczynski, also known as the "Unabomber", who was responsible for planting or mailing 16 bombs in the United States over a period of nearly 18 years, killing three people and wounding 23 others. Kaczynski's social and political views appear closest to anarchism and contain elements of Luddism, in that he rails against technology, modernity and the destruction of the environment. Kaczynski [14, 15] states that the continued scientific and technical progress of society would inevitably result in the extinction of individual liberty. In his 1995 manifesto entitled "Industrial Society and Its Future", Kaczynski [14, p. 1] argues:

> Industrial Revolution and its consequences have been a disaster for the human race. They have greatly increased the life-expectancy of those of us who live in 'advanced' countries, but they have destabilized society, have made life unfulfilling, have subjected human beings to indignities, have led to widespread psychological suffering... and have inflicted severe damage on the natural world. The continued development of technology will worsen the situation.

In his 35,000-word manifesto, Kaczynski [14, p. 15] further notes that industrial-technological society "cannot be reformed in such a way as to prevent it from progressively narrowing the sphere of human freedom". Kaczynski condemns "leftism" as "anti-individualistic" and "pro-collectivist", opposing it to what he envisioned as anarchy, which would leave people "able to control the circumstances of their own lives" [14, p. 38]. Further, he claims that the anarchist rejects technology, "because it makes small groups dependent on large organizations" [14, p. 38].

Kaczynski's public statements present justifications for his actions. In his manifesto he writes that "in order to get our message before the public with some chance of making a lasting impression, we've had to kill people" [14, p. 16].[7] On another occasion, Kaczynski [16, A01] says that "people who wilfully and knowingly promote economic growth and technical progress, in our eyes they are

[7] Please note the use of the term "we" here. In his writings Kaczynski regularly referred to "we" or to a fictitious group called "FC" (Freedom Club), but he acted alone.

criminals, and if they get blown up they deserve it". During his trial, Kaczynski justifies his bombing campaign as "an attempt to slow the march of technology blindly crushing man's freedom" [17]. It has been argued that Kaczynski may also have been inspired by the radical fringe of the environmentalist movement [18]. In 1994, Kaczynski reportedly attended a meeting of environmentalists at the University of Montana [19]. At that meeting speakers suggested that public relations firm Burson-Marsteller had designed the public relations campaign for Exxon following the Exxon Valdez incident, in which a tanker ran aground and spilled oil in Alaska in 1989. One month later, Kaczynski killed Thomas Mosser, an advertising executive at Young & Rubicam, the parent company of Burson-Marsteller. A letter from the Unabomber, excerpts of which were published in the *The New York Times* in April 1995, said that Mosser had been killed because his company had helped Exxon clean up its public image. However, Kaczynski's former classmate Alston Chase [20] strongly disputes that Kaczynski was an environmentalist, arguing that he only pretended to be one in order to recruit environmentalists into his campaign.

Kaczynski's political motives are inextricably related to personal resentment. He describes his perceived social rejection and that organized society frustrated his urge for physical freedom and personal autonomy. It is likely that over the years Kaczynski increasingly attributed his personal frustrations to external factors, leading him to develop a deep-seated hatred toward modern society in general. In his journal [21] he writes:

> What makes a situation intolerable is the fact that in all probability, the values that I detest, will soon be achieved through science, an utterly complete and permanent victory throughout the whole world, with a total extrication of everything I value. Through super human computers and mind control there simply will be no place for a rebellious person to hide and my kind of people will vanish forever from the earth. It's not merely the fact that I cannot fit into society that has induced me to rebel, as violently as I have, it is the fact that I can see society made possible by science inexorably imposing on me.

Although Kaczynski principally targeted individuals and organizations that he held responsible for scientific and technological progress and the destruction of individual freedom and the environment, his resentment also appears to have been related to his personal situation: his perceived dysfunction in life, particularly his inability to establish a relationship with a female [21, 22].

The case of Theodore Kaczynski indicates that political, ideological and individual influences often intertwine in complex ways and can be subject to change over time. Despite the vast differences in the professed ideologies of Franz Fuchs and Kaczynski, Fuchs' lone wolf operations should also be understood in this way. Fuchs was responsible for a bombing campaign in Austria and Germany that lasted for nearly 4 years between 1993 and 1996. His bomb attacks killed four people and injured 15 others, principally targeting immigrants as well as organizations and individuals who Fuchs considered to be "friendly to foreigners" (e.g. [23]). Fuchs expressed himself, and was characterized in the media, as xenophobic and racist. In his letters, Fuchs mentions the discrimination of German Austrians and urges the government to alter its immigration policy. However, whilst his statements and target selection are consistent with a right-wing ideology, there is confusion about Fuchs's exact motives, and it is clear that he acted out of a combination of personal and political motives. In Fuchs' case, it seems that personal resentment was at least equally dominant in his violent radicalization as his espoused ideological or political causes. Indeed, Fuchs was characterized by profound self-hate and an accumulated hatred of the outside world. Although his attacks were principally directed at foreigners and related organizations and individuals, Fuchs's hatred of the outside world seems to have been more all-encompassing, leading him to live in reclusion. His trial focused almost exclusively on this personal aspect of the bombing campaign—portraying Fuchs as a mentally ill and socially inept loner—leaving the political dimension of the attacks out of consideration. However, Fuchs himself never provided a coherent statement of his purpose and motive following his arrest in 1997, and many questions surrounding his exact motivation remain unanswered [23, 24].

Despite its vastly different cultural and political context, Yigal Amir's assassination of the Israeli Prime Minister Yitzhak Rabin on 4 November 1995 also fits into this broad framework. Rabin was shot when walking back to his car after a pro-peace rally in Tel Aviv and succombed to his injuries while in surgery at Ichilov Hospital. His killer, 25-year-old Jewish male Yigal Amir, justified his deed with Jewish theology, historical precedents and biblical examples, stating that he "acted alone on God's orders" and had no regrets [25].

Although Amir operated alone, his act was preceded by an unparalleled campaign of delegitimation of the Israeli government and character assassination of Rabin and Foreign Minister Shimon Peres by Israel's far right [26–29]. This campaign was triggered by the ratification of the 1993 Oslo Accords with the Palestine Liberation Organization (PLO) and a series of Palestinian terrorist attacks on Israeli territory. Not only did Israel's ultranationalists portray the democratically elected government as illegitimate, but its leaders began to be labelled as "traitors" and "collaborators with terrorism" [26, pp. 4–5]. The radicalization of Israel's far right culminated in the 1994 Hebron massacre in which Baruch Goldstein, a fierce opponent of the peace process, singlehandedly killed 29 Muslims and wounded more than 100 others. The Hebron massacre was a milestone for Yigal Amir. He admired Goldstein and is said to have decided at Goldstein's funeral that he also had to conduct an "exemplary act" [30, p. 124]. From that morning onward, Amir concentrated his efforts on achieving the "spiritual readiness" that Goldstein had displayed [27]. As Karpin and Friedman [27] argue, Amir too aspired to be an agent of God, an emissary of his people.

Amir convinced himself that he was on a divine mission and that in killing Rabin he was acting in accordance with Jewish religious law (*Halakha*) [26]. Days after his arrest, Amir stated to reporters that the Israeli government was surrendering the biblical heritage of the Jews and betraying settlers in the West Bank, and that the new Palestinian autonomy taking shape in once-occupied lands put Israel in great danger [31]. He was convinced that in order to save the nation, Rabin had to die: "Maybe physically I acted alone, but what pulled the trigger was not only my finger, but the finger of this whole nation, which for 2,000 years yearned for this land and dreamed of it" [32].

The above indicates that Amir's religious and political views were inspired and shared by a small but significant section of the Israeli far right. However, it later became clear that there may have been other dimensions to his deed. For example, it has been shown that Amir was involved in a struggle for personal excellence and fame, and had a strong desire to prove his strength of will to others. Amir was also found to suffer from a depressive personality which preceded his act and which may have contributed to his violent radicalization (e.g. [26]). Amir was reportedly devastated when the relationship with his girlfriend was broken off in early 1995, leading him to plunge back into his grim plans with single-minded vigor [28].

Finally, let us briefly consider here the case of David Copeland, who was responsible for three bombings targeting London's Black, Asian and gay communities. Police interviews with Copeland and subsequent court reports provide insight into his motivations for the attacks, revealing a combination of political and personal motives. First and foremost, Copeland framed his actions in terms of an extreme-right ideology, describing his overall aim as being "to spread fear, resentment and hatred throughout this country" [33]. He went on to argue: "My aim was political. It was to cause a racial war in this country" [34]. When asked what he believed in, he stated: "I am a national socialist, or Nazi, whatever you want to call me. I believe in a ruling master race; I believe in race and country first, with the white race as the master race and Aryan domination of the world" [33]. Copeland thought the bombs would ignite a full-blown racial war in the United Kingdom [35]. He also hoped that they would create a major backlash among ethnic minorities. At times Copeland hinted at a religious motive, although his statements on this issue are inconsistent and contradictory. A psychiatrist who interviewed Copeland said that he "described being controlled by God when carrying out the bombings" [33]. On another occasion, Copeland admits: "I am not a religious person, but I believe in God and regard the Bible as against racial mixing" [33].

Whilst these statements clearly indicate Copeland's right-wing and racist beliefs, some of his other statements highlight that he wanted notoriety. Much like Yigal Amir, Copeland emphasized how "I wanted to be famous… I believe in what I believe in and I took that belief to the extreme" [36]. He stated that he wanted to cause "murder, mayhem, chaos, damage—to get on the news as the top story, really" [36]. When asked whether he sought to evade police while carrying the bombs, he responded: "Personally I wanted to get caught… To be famous in some sort of way… If no one remembers who you were, you never existed" [36, 37]. In addition to right-wing and neo-Nazi literature, police found newspaper cuttings, pictures and other items relating to his own bombings in Copeland's flat. Copeland said he felt "exhilarated" by the media coverage of his actions and "cheated" when the right-wing organizations Combat 18 and White Wolves began to claim responsibility. He stated: "I planned this. I have been dreaming about it for ages—doing what I did, getting caught, going to court—it is my destiny" [38].

He called the groups that claimed responsibility for the Brixton bombing "a bunch of yobs" trying to take his glory [39].

Another personal motive that appears to have played a major role in Copeland's targeting of the gay community was his personal hatred of gay men. Copeland claimed to have developed this hatred during his childhood in reaction to his parents who allegedly subjected him to humiliation and mental torture as a child. On this matter, Buncombe [40] hypothesizes that Copeland meant that he felt his parents had wanted a girl and/or that they were suspicious that he was homosexual. Copeland did not elaborate on this issue; however, he did express that "I'm just very homophobic … I just hate them", and described homosexuals as "perverted degenerates who were no use to society and should be put to death" [35]. "Even as a racist, I would prefer the company of a black or Asian to a gay white man", he reportedly told police [33].

In sum, the case studies illustrate how lone wolf terrorists tend to create their own ideologies that combine broader political, religious or social aims with personal frustrations and aversion. It can be unclear which motive—if any—predominates. Furthermore, the motivational patterns of lone wolf terrorists tend to shift over time as their radicalization progresses (or de-escalates), depending in part on their interaction with significant others such as communities of support. These findings underline the point made earlier that typologies or profiles based on static ideal types of ideology or motivation are problematic because many lone wolf terrorists do not easily fit in them. Moreover, whilst exposure to ideologies justifying terrorism is a key ingredient in the violent radicalization of individual activists [41], the espousal of a particular ideology alone does not guarantee that radicalization towards terrorist violence will ensue [42]. It is imperative to examine the other factors and influences that affect the violent radicalization of lone wolf terrorists. It is to this issue that I will now turn.

References

1. Department of Homeland Security (2009) Rightwing extremism: current economic and political climate fueling resurgence in radicalization and recruitment. DHS, Washington
2. Pantucci R (2011) A typology of lone wolves: preliminary analysis of lone islamist terrorists. ICSR, London
3. Public Prosecution of the Netherlands (2003) Closing speech public prosecutor, 1 April. http://www.om.nl/dossier/de_zaak_fortuyn/_de_zaak_fortuyn_nieuwsberichten/21709/. Accessed 3 May 2007
4. Stolwijk E (2003) De zaak moord op Pim Fortuyn. Opportuun, April. http://www.om.nl/algemene_onderdelen/uitgebreid_zoeken/@122772/de_zaak_moord_op_pim/. Accessed 2 Aug 2008
5. de Jong S, Niemöller J (2003) Volkert's verborgen verleden. HP/De Tijd, pp 26–36 (4 July)
6. de Jong S, Niemöller J (2003) Raadsels rond het Volkert-proces. HP/De Tijd, pp 20–26 (25 July)
7. Spaaij R (2010) The enigma of lone wolf terrorism: an assessment. Stud Confl Terrorism 33(9):854–870

8. Stern J (2003) Terror in the name of God: why religious militants kill. HarperCollins, New York
9. Schuster H, Stone C (2005) Hunting Eric Rudolph. Berkley Books, New York
10. Vollers M (2006) Lone wolf: Eric Rudolph: murder myth, and the pursuit of an American outlaw. HarperCollins, New York
11. Homans C (2011) Norway's 9/11? Foreign Policy, 22 July. http://www.foreignpolicy.com/articles/2011/07/22/norways_911?print=yes&hidecomments=yes&page=full. Accessed 24 July 2011
12. Hegghammer T (2011) The rise of the macro-nationalists. The New York Times, 30 July, SR5. http://www.nytimes.com/2011/07/31/opinion/sunday/the-rise-of-the-macro-nationalists.html. Accessed 3 Aug 2011
13. Roy O (2004) Globalized islam: the search for a new ummah. Columbia University Press, New York
14. Kaczynski T (1995) Industrial society and its future (unabomber's manifesto). http://www.provokateur.com/webres/Unabomber%20Manifesto%20by%20Theodore%20Kaczynski. Accessed 8 June 2007
15. Kaczynski T (2002) Hit where it hurts. Green Anarchy 8(Spring). http://www.godlikeproductions.com/forum1/message488697/pg1. Accessed 4 June 2007
16. Kurtz H (1995) Unabomber manifesto is published: public safety reasons cited in joint decision by post, N.Y. times. The Washington Post, 19 Sept, A01
17. MacFarquhar N (1996) A luddite's high-tech plea. The New York Times, 15 Dec
18. Arnold R (1997) Ecoterror: the violent agenda to save nature: the world of the Unabomber. Free Enterprise Press, Washington
19. Kushner H (2003) Encyclopedia of terrorism. Sage, Thousand Oaks
20. Chase A (2003) Harvard and the unabomber: the education of an American terrorist. W.W. Norton, New York
21. Johnson SC (1998) Psychological evaluation of Theodore John Kaczynski. Federal Correctional Institution Butner, North Carolina
22 Springer N (2009) Patterns of radicalization: Identifying the markers and warning signs of domestic lone wolf terrorists in our midst. Unpublished Master's thesis. Monterey, CA: Naval Postgraduate School
23. Friedrichsen G (1999) Nur irgendein Kasperl? Der Spiegel, pp 184–186 (22 Feb)
24. Scheid HC (2001) Franz Fuchs: Doch kein Einzeltäter?. Styria Verlag, Graz
25. Lewis A, (1995) On God's orders. The New York Times, 6 Nov
26. Sprinzak E (1999) Brother against brother: violence and extremism in Israeli politics from Altalena to the Rabin assassination. The Free Press, New York
27. Karpin M, Friedman I (1998) Murder in the name of God: the plot to kill Yitzhak Rabin. Henry Holt and Co, New York
28. Kifner J (1995) Belief to blood: the making of Rabin's killer. The New York Times, 19 Nov
29. Friedman TL (1995) Land or life?. The New York Times, 19 Nov
30. Sprinzak E (2000) Israel's radical right and the countdown to the Rabin assassination. In: Peri Y (ed) The assassination of Yitzhak Rabin. Stanford University Press, Stanford, pp 96–128
31. Schmemann S (1995) Rabin is laid to rest, mourned by Israel and the world. The New York Times, 7 Nov
32. Greenberg J (1995) Rabin's killer says he acted for past generations of Jews. The New York Times, 21 Nov
33. Clough S (2000) Nail bomber tried to start 'a race war'. The Daily Telegraph, 6 June
34. Hari J (2009) The looming threat of terror that comes from the far right. The Independent, 14 Oct. http://www.independent.co.uk/opinion/commentators/johann-hari/johann-hari-the-looming-threat-of-terror-that-comes-from-the-far-right-1802167.html. Accessed 7 Aug 2011
35. Hopkins N (2000) The bomber who tried to unleash a race war. The Guardian, 6 June
36. Clough S (2000) Soho nail bomber told police it was his destiny to cause death. The Daily Telegraph, 7 June

37. Bennetto J (2000) Police took just 14 days to track down nail bomber. The Independent, 30 June
38. Hall S (2000) Bomber 'exhilarated' by media spotlight. The Guardian, 13 June
39. Clough S (2000) Secrets of a loner's bedsit. The Daily Telegraph, 6 June
40. Buncombe A (2000) A man sexually confused and obsessed with the far right. The Independent, 30 June
41. Turk A (2008) Sociology of terrorism. In: Matson R (ed) The spirit of sociology: a reader. Pearson, Boston, pp 490–502
42. Reinares F, Alonso R, Bjørgo T, Della Porta D, Coolsaet R, Khosrokhavar F, Lohlker R, Ranstorp M, Schmid A, Silke A, Taarnby M, de Vries G (2008) Radicalisation processes leading to acts of terrorism: European Commission Expert Group on Violent Radicalisation, Brussels
43. Metzger T (n.d.) Begin with lone wolves. http://www.resist.com/Articles/literature/BeginWithLoneWolvesByTomMetzger.htm. Accessed 15 August 2011
44. Metzger T (n.d.) Laws for the lone wolf. http://www.resist.com/Articles/literature/LawsForTheLoneWolfByTomMetzger.htm. Accessed 15 August 2011

Chapter 6
Influences and Radicalization

6.1 Theorizing Radicalization

How and why do individuals become lone wolf terrorists? What are the factors that affect a person's attitudes and behaviour to the extent that violent radicalization and, ultimately, lone wolf terrorism is the outcome? Although the motivational patterns and ideological sources discussed in the previous chapter go some way to answering these questions, in order to attain a deeper understanding of lone wolf terrorism, radicalization should be understood in a broader sense, that is, as a complex, dynamic, multidimensional and phased process.

Violent radicalization can be defined as "the process of adopting or promoting an extremist belief system for the purpose of facilitating ideologically based violence to advance political, religious, or social change" [1, p. 2]. Violent radicalization is only at the far end of a wide repertoire of possible radical expressions, of course, and the number of people who choose violence as their preferred method is extremely low [2]. The key to explaining the socialization of lone wolf terrorists, then, is understanding how these individuals are brought to the point where they see themselves as bearers of the responsibility for, or a vanguard of, violent actions [3].

In recent decades there has been a major upsurge in research into violent radicalization. This literature greatly enhances our knowledge of the factors and influences that shape radicalization into terrorism. It shows, for example, that there is no single explanation or pattern of radicalization and that violent radicalization involves a complex interplay of macro-, meso- and micro-level factors and mechanisms [2, 4–14]. Thus, violent radicalization takes places at the intersection of an enabling environment and individual trajectories towards greater militancy. Although violent radicalization generally "thrives in an enabling environment that is characterized by a more widely shared sense of injustice, exclusion and humiliation (real or perceived) among the constituencies the terrorists claim to represent", not all individuals who share this sense of injustice or are living in the same polarized environment turn to radicalism and even less so to terrorism

R. Spaaij, *Understanding Lone Wolf Terrorism*, SpringerBriefs in Criminology,
DOI: 10.1007/978-94-007-2981-0_6, © The Author(s) 2012

[2, p.17]. Concrete personal experiences, kinship and friendship, as well as group dynamics and socialization into the use of violence are "critical in triggering the actual process of radicalization escalating to engagement in acts of terrorism" [2, p. 18]. In this context, Della Porta [15] proposes an analytical model for explaining political violence in which environmental conditions, group dynamics, and individual motivations and circumstances are all taken into account. Most theories of radicalization view feelings of discontent and adversity/deprivation—what can be called the "instrumental motive" which is affected by broader political, economic and social conditions–as a platform for stepping initially onto the path to political radicalization. However, only very few people come to resist a perceived injustice through violent action [5, 6].

One of the most original sociological explanations of how people become radicalized into violent extremism and terrorism has been developed by Michel Wieviorka. Wieviorka [16, p. x] argues that in order to understand terrorism, "one must begin at the bottom with the social and cultural meanings of action as they are transformed, distorted, and also recomposed in the trajectories of the actors". For Wieviorka, the violence which terrorists use is a substitute for the relationship they once shared with the constituencies on whose behalf they claim to be fighting. He shows how terrorism can be understood as the final outcome of a process of inversion concerning three fundamental dimensions of a social movement: identity, opposition and totality. In this paradigm, the principle of identity, which defines the actor and the constituency on whose behalf he or she speaks, ceases to be a reference to any real social entity and instead comes to champion some mythic or abstract entity, essence or symbol (e.g. an abstract notion of justice, morality or freedom). This inversion of identity results in an "aggravated subjectivism" in which the terrorist defines himself or herself primarily through a total commitment to the cause for which he or she is the self-proclaimed vanguard and the consciousness of all who have been alienated or who remain unconscious of the historical role they have to play [16, p. 8]. Thus, the principle of opposition that defines the social adversary undergoes an objectivization of the enemy, in which society and state are fused together into a single, all-consuming threat, and the enemy is transformed into a concrete target to attack or a system to annihilate. The principle of totality then ceases to be a common reference to a given cause and no longer fuels new future-directed actions. Where there had once been a common ground on which political differences could be resolved, now all that remains is a need to overthrow the present system. The principle of totality dissolves into a life-or-death combat that calls for the destruction of the existing order [16].

Like most theories of radicalization into terrorism, Wieviorka focuses predominantly on the group and interpersonal dimensions of violent radicalization as well as the wider political and cultural conditions that affect these dimensions. This raises the question of whether such analytical models can also help explain terrorism carried out by lone individuals who are not part of a terrorist group. The answer to this question should be "yes", as long as the analysis takes into consideration how external conditions and group influences affect *individual* beliefs and behaviours. Moreover, it must account for the specific circumstances and personal characteristics of the individuals involved and their interaction with significant others, such as family, peers, radical ideologues, extremist movements and virtual communities. Put differently, individual terrorists are "subject to an array of influences related to self-perception, family, community and identity" [17, p. 16].

Whilst lone wolf terrorism results from solitary action during which the direct support or command of others is absent, such action and its justification does not take place in a vacuum. As noted in Chap. 5, exposure to ideologies justifying terrorism is a key ingredient in the mix of personal and vicarious learning experiences leading to a commitment to terrorism [3]. The available evidence indicates that there is a variable degree of interaction with extremist movements among lone wolf terrorists, if only tacitly through the creation of a wider supportive community promoting terrorist violence [18, 19]. The analytical distinction between lone wolf terrorism and group-based terrorism is often problematic in practice because inter-group dynamics typically also influence lone individuals, for example in their framing of grievances and justifications for violence against the enemy. Conversely, lone wolf terrorists can also influence larger movements. The actions of David Copeland and Yigal Amir, for instance, were supported by a section of symphatizers from affiliated ideological milieus that portrayed them as martyrs for their cause. British neo-Nazi Neil Lewington reportedly sought to emulate Copeland and Timothy McVeigh, and kept videos detailing their attacks at his home (see Appendix). As described below, Copeland himself was inspired by Eric Rudolph's bombing attack during the 1996 Atlanta Olympic Games. Let us examine here the key patterns of violent radicalization as they relate to lone wolf terrorism, commencing with personal circumstances and then moving to interpersonal relations and sociocultural and political influences.

6.2 Personal Circumstances and Social Backgrounds

What psychological factors motivate the lone wolf terrorist and influence his or her perceptions and self-identity? As noted, there is no single personality type or profile of the lone wolf terrorist. Furthermore, personality traits alone are not very good predictors of behaviour [20]. Scholars such as Post [21] and Horgan [22] argue that, overall, terrorists should not be regarded as suffering from any identifiable psychopathology. In the same vein, Crenshaw [23, p. 99] notes that "the outstanding common characteristic [of terrorists] is normality. Terrorism often seems to be the connecting link among dissimilar personalities". Similarly, Reinares et al. [2, p. 9] stress that those who engage in terrorist activity "are not mentally disturbed people" and "are essentially unremarkable in psychological terms".

The question then is whether these observations are transferable to lone wolf terrorists. Hewitt [24] argues that although most terrorists are, psychologically speaking, "normal", the rate of psychological disturbance is higher among lone wolves. Pantucci [25] also notes that mental problems or a general social inability underlie the histories of relatively many lone wolf terrorists. My own research supports the conclusion that, in comparison with group-actor terrorism, lone wolves tend to have a greater propensity to suffer mental health issues [18, 26]. Although precision here is difficult, lone wolf terrorists seem relatively likely to suffer from some form of psychological disturbance. For example, as discussed below, four of the five lone wolf terrorists in the case studies were diagnosed with some form of personality disorder. Four out of five also appear to have experienced depression during at least one stage of their lives (all but Copeland), though this was not systematically assessed in all cases [26]. (Copeland and Kaczynski were also diagnosed with schizophrenia, but this diagnosis is contested.) At least some of the other lone wolf terrorists in the database are also believed to suffer from psychological disturbance (cf. [25]).

Moreover, as described in detail below, lone wolf terrorists often display a degree of social ineffectiveness and social alienation [18] which may also be viewed as symptoms of psychological abnormality. Those individuals who yearned to be a member of a group often found in the end that they had difficulty being accepted, feeling a part of, or succeeding in a group [27]. In some cases lone wolf terrorists even exhibit the desire to withdraw themselves from mainstream society and from wider communities and act completely on their own. Importantly, however, the nature of the psychological disorder or social ineffectiveness typically does not cause lone wolf terrorists to become cognitively disorganized, and in most cases they do not fully lose contact with reality (cf. [28]). Indeed, all five individuals in the case studies planned and executed their attacks in a logical and rational way.

Volkert van der Graaf experienced depression in his mid-twenties, especially after his first girlfriend broke off their relationship. Van der Graaf attempted to commit suicide but failed and, according to the psychiatrist who evaluated him, this was followed by an attempt to buy drugs for a second suicide attempt. He subsequently tried to find self-confidence and self-identity in ideology and moral principles [29]. Van der Graaf was also diagnosed with a personality disorder, although the court ruled that this condition played no part in his assassination of Pim Fortuyn and that van der Graaf was fully "sane" [30]. In a similar vein, in his mid-twenties Franz Fuchs became severely depressed and eventually planned to commit suicide following his failure to find challenging employment or a partner. On 8 August 1976, Fuchs wrote to his parents: "My meaning and existence for mankind is zero" [31]. His father had him admitted into a psychiatric hospital. Fuchs was released after two months and declared recovered. According to Böhmer [32], Fuchs suffered from obsessive–compulsive disorder; however, this was not systematically diagnosed after his arrest.

After his arrest, David Copeland claimed that he had been having sadistic dreams from the age of 12, citing difficulties concentrating and sleeping. A year earlier he was prescribed mild anti-depressants to help him cope with anxiety attacks. Copeland appears to have been suffering from some form of mental illness, but the nature and severity of his condition is contested. Five defense psychiatrists reportedly concluded that he was suffering from schizophrenia. One of them stated that the visions Copeland spoke of as a teenager were consistent with the first stages of a schizophrenic condition. This diagnosis was challenged by the prosecutors who were unimpressed by his claim of diminished responsibility [33]. Another consultant psychiatrist concluded that Copeland was not suffering from schizophrenia but did have a minor personality disorder that was not serious enough for him to avoid a murder charge [34].

Theodore Kaczynski also had a history of brief contacts with mental health organizations. While studying at the University of Michigan he sought psychiatric contact after he had been experiencing weeks of intense and persistent sexual excitement involving fantasies of being a female. Kaczynski seriously contemplated undergoing a sex-change operation [35], and recounts that he was aware that this would require a psychiatric referral and made an appointment at the university's health center [36]. He later described feeling rage, shame and humiliation over his attempt to seek psychiatric evaluation, noting it as a significant turning point in his life [36]. Kaczynski also indicated that he suffered from severe depression for at least a number of months in the late 1980s, which affected him to some degree until 1994. During his trial Kaczynski insisted that his defense not be based on the claim of mental illness. The official psychiatric evaluation was inconclusive on this matter. While Kaczynski was found competent to stand trial, psychiatrist Dr Sally Johnson [36] stated that he was probably a paranoid schizophrenic preoccupied with two main delusional beliefs: that he was being controlled by modern technology, and that his dysfunction in life (e.g. his inability to establish a relationship with a female) was a direct result of psychological abuse by his parents. Critics contest this assessment by arguing that there is no substantive evidence that Kaczynski was mentally ill or "out of touch with reality" apart from his unconventional social and political views [24].

As noted above, a significant pattern of commonality is that lone wolf terrorists tend to display a (varying) degree of social ineffectiveness and social alienation [18]. Those lone wolves who yearned to be a member of a group often found in the end that they had difficulty being accepted, feeling a part of, or succeeding in a group. Thus, a number of lone wolves developed an isolationist attitude which led them to act on their own. Springer [37] attributes the initial cultivation of an isolationist attitude to the conditions surrounding childhood and adolescent years, asserting that the three terrorists he studied (Kaczynski, Rudolph and McVeigh) spent a lot of time by themselves and struggled to establish and maintain intimate human relationships (e.g. female companionship). They increasingly "isolated themselves, cut off contact with their families and began to stew. Once in isolation, their ideologies would take shape and slowly inch them closer to the line of direct action, violence in the name of their ideologies" [37, p. 79]. Springer [37, p. 72] concludes that "their isolationism, lack of group acceptance or success within a group, and difficulty establishing emotional connections led each of them viewing themselves as the ultimate loners" who became increasingly focused on their ideologies and, eventually, violent action.

Although no single profile exists, the case studies also demonstrate that lone wolf terrorists tend to be social isolates who generally feel more comfortable on their own, albeit with significant variations. Only Volkert van der Graaf was living with a partner (who is also the mother of his daughter) at the time of the attack, while the other four men were not in a relationship over the times of their attacks. Two of them, Franz Fuchs and Theodore Kaczynski, lived in reclusion and shunned most forms of direct contact with the outside world. Whilst living in reclusion, they planned and began to take revenge for the perceived injustices and humiliations they had experienced. After leaving his job at the University of California in 1969, Theodore Kaczynski spent approximately two years attempting to locate a piece of land upon which he could live in isolation from society. In 1971 he built a small cabin on a piece of wilderness land near Lincoln, Montana. From 1971 to his arrest in 1996 he lived a solitary life in the cabin, except for some short periods of time when he travelled and sought temporary employment to earn some money. He made an effort to live off the land and gradually developed the necessary skills in tool making, gardening, food preservation and hunting. Kaczynski wrote in his journal that he did not, nor did he want to, fit into organized society. His move to Lincoln was a way of escaping from modern society [36]. Similarly, Franz Fuchs also increasingly lived in reclusion and had very little or no contact with family and friends. He developed a deep-seated hatred towards the outside world and regarded himself as a failure [31, 38]. Fuchs increasingly formulated his resentment towards immigrants and the immigration policy of the Austrian government and in December 1993, began to put his frustrations into practice through bomb attacks.

With the exception of Volkert van der Graaf, who had been a member of a number of organizations, none of the five lone wolf terrorists studied appear to have felt particularly comfortable in organized groups. These individuals' preference to act alone and their feelings of discomfort regarding membership of an organized extremist group go some way to explain why lone wolves often stay lone wolves. Copeland and Amir did try to engage with like-minded individuals by joining a political party or extremist group for some time. In 1997 Copeland joined the British National Party (BNP) and acted as a steward at some BNP meetings. He soon abandoned the party because of his disappointment that the BNP did not advocate violence. Back in Hampshire, he joined a small neo-Nazi organization, the National Socialist Movement, where he later became a regional unit leader only weeks before the start of his bombing campaign [39]. Copeland's case highlights that even though lone wolf terrorists are not members of a terrorist group, they may identify or sympathize with a larger movement or have previously been a member or affiliate of such a movement. As noted in Chap. 3, there are interesting parallels with the accused Norwegian lone wolf Anders Breivik here, who was a member of Norway's Progress Party but left because in his view the party did not go far enough.

In addition to their diverse personalities, lone wolf terrorists exhibit a variety of social backgrounds. It is possible, however, to identify a fairly common pattern among lone wolf terrorists: with significant variations, they are more often than not relatively well educated and relatively socially advantaged. This finding is consistent with what we know about terrorists in general, namely that terrorism is more frequently associated with relative affluence and social advantage rather than lack of education, poverty or other indicators of deprivation [3].

The case studies illustrate this point. Four of the five lone wolf terrorists were recognized as intelligent or highly intelligent persons (all but Copeland). Yigal Amir was born in 1970 to a middle-class Israeli family, and attended a highly respected school, the Hesder Yeshiva of Kerem de-Yavneh, which was known for the relative moderation of its instructors and graduates [40]. As discussed below, Amir's political views became more radical during his tenure at Bar Ilan University, where he studied law and computer science and was recognized as a very good student [41]. Franz Fuchs was recognized early in life for his exceptional intelligence, being especially skilled in physics and reportedly outperforming his teachers on many subjects. Fuchs later studied theoretical physics at the University of Graz and had the potential to develop an academic career; however, he decided to abandon his studies because he could "not bear the miserable student life" [31]. He accepted a position at a Mercedes factory in Germany, where he worked as an assembly line employee. Volkert van der Graaf was also described as an intellectually gifted individual, was raised in a middle-class family and considered to be a good student during secondary school. Van der Graaf later moved to Wageningen to study environmental hygiene at the Wageningen agricultural university; however, he failed to complete his studies, opting instead to devote his time to protecting the environment [42]. During this period van der Graaf's beliefs concerning animal rights and environmental protection became more rigid and he developed a pessimistic worldview.

Theodore Kaczynski was born in Chicago in 1942 to lower-middle-class parents. His family moved several times, gradually bettering their housing status. They eventually settled in the middle-class suburb of Evergreen Park, Illinois, in the early 1950s. A highly intelligent student, Kaczynski twice skipped a grade in school. He later described skipping a grade in elementary school as a pivotal event in his life that caused the underdevelopment of his social skills. He recalled not fitting in with the older children and increasingly being the subject of verbal abuse and bullying [36]. At age 16 Kaczynski became a mathematics student at Harvard University, graduating in 1962. By age 25 he had completed his PhD and was highly rated by his academic supervisors. He accepted a position as assistant professor in mathematics at the University of California at Berkeley, a position he held until June 1969.

I should reiterate here that, despite the identified patterns of commonality discussed above, there is no single profile of what "makes" a person become a lone wolf terrorist. Individuals involved in terrorism are influenced by various combinations of motivations and undergo rather different processes of violent radicalization [2]. The radicalization process, then, should be viewed as consisting of a complex and dynamic set of circumstances and mechanisms that shape the individual's "causal story" and is arguably unique for each individual [43, p. 139]. Certain life experiences, such as histories of abuse (real or imagined) during childhood or damaging home environments, are relatively commonly found in terrorist biographies, and the case studies provide some examples of such experiences. David Copeland, for instance, claimed that his parents psychologically abused him as a child, whereas Theodore Kaczynki's parents put immense academic pressure on him, allegedly causing him to slip into isolation and become a consummate loner [37]. However, as Borum [20] notes, none of these experiences contribute significantly to a causal explanation of terrorism.

6.3 Sociocultural and Political Influences

In Chap. 3, I argue that many of the actions that appear to be lone wolf ventures have broader ideologies of validation and communities of belief behind them (see also [44]). Lone wolf terrorists are more often than not strongly influenced (if only tacitly or vicariously) by wider communities that provide ideologies which cultivate a sustained, alternate sense of morality capable of justifying the destruction of life and property that terrorism entails [19]. They often draw on such ideologies of validation to frame a particular grievance as an injustice and to place blame on a certain group of people, state or government. In the psychological literature this is referred to as the mechanism of externalization: the channeling of personal frustrations and the attribution of responsibility for all perceived problems (e.g. an unfolding crisis or deeply corrupted society) to the Other [21]. The vilification or demonization of the enemy can drive an impetus for aggressive or violent action to defend the aggrieved or remedy the wrong [20]. Social identification with broader political, social or religious struggles (real or imagined) encourages the lone wolf terrorist's dualistic categorization of the world into "us" and "them", thus stereotyping social groups and dehumanizing the enemy, and effectively weakening psychological barriers against violence [45]. As noted earlier, lone wolf terrorists may not only internalize such dualistic categorizations but also, to varying extents, physically withdraw themselves from mainstream society.

The case studies illustrate how communities of support may be engaged with in multiple ways. First of all, this can be achieved through direct contact with like-minded individuals and groups. In cases where lone wolf terrorists strongly identify with an existing movement or have been directly involved in such a movement, their personalized ideologies may closely reflect the political, social or religious aims of these movements. David Copeland, for example, made an attempt to align himself with an extremist milieu that conformed to his expectations of a violent, revolutionary vanguard by connecting with the BNP and the National Socialist Movement. His right-wing connections augmented his personal worldview that "regarded mainstream society as a corrupt and decaying order, in need of violent confrontation" [19]. As noted in Chap. 5, Copeland justified his actions using extreme-right ideology, asserting that his intent was "to spread fear, resentment and hatred throughout this country, it was to cause a racial war" [46].

He went on to assert: "I am a national socialist, or Nazi, whatever you want to call me. I believe in a ruling master race … Aryan domination of the world" [46]. Moreover, the influence of the American far right on his personalized ideology is evident, *inter alia*, in his racist obsessions and his statement that "ZOG", the "Zionist Occupation Government"—a term often used by American White supremacists—was trying to sweep him under the carpet by pumping him full of drugs [39].

The case of Yigal Amir further illustrates how lone wolf terrorists may engage with extremist movements. Amir grew up in a heavily politicized environment characterized by a growing polarization between the more moderate sections of Israeli nationalists and the far right on the issue of how to deal with the Israeli-Palestinian conflict. Amir's mother was known for extremist views which she expressed, for instance, by making a pilgrimage to the grave of Baruch Goldstein [40]. However, although both his parents supported the idea of Greater Israel, they reportedly "preached brotherhood and unity, and said Jews should not fight one another" [47]. In the years leading up to the attack, Amir's worldview radicalized significantly, including not only a fierce hatred of Muslims but also a growing distrust of the Israeli government. Amir obtained military experience in the Golani Brigade, a combat unit in the Israeli Defense Forces, and it is reported that while in military service he tortured local Palestinians and took pride in his deeds [40]. Amir later returned to Herzliya to study at Bar Ilan University, where he devoted much of his time to the study of Jewish religious law and right-wing political activities [41, 47]. Amir also participated in the events organized by Zo Artzenu, a right-wing movement that was instrumental in intensifying the atmosphere of delegitimation surrounding the Israeli government. During these events participants vented their frustrations and shared struggle experiences. Some of them spoke and chanted freely about the need to execute the "traitors", referring to Yitzhak Rabin and Shimon Peres [40].

Let us also consider the case of Volkert van der Graaf. Most of the organizations in which van der Graaf participated were relatively moderate in their views on animal rights and environmental protection. He engaged with animal rights activists from an early age, for example through his membership of the Dutch WWF youth movement and his employment at a bird sanctuary in Walcheren [48]. Van der Graaf's worldview gradually became more radical after he moved to Wageningen to commence his undergraduate degree. During this period he participated in a number of moderate and more radical environmental and animal protection organizations. Van der Graaf later co-founded the animal rights group Vereniging Milieuoffensief (Environmental Offensive Association; VMO) which conducted more than 2,000 legal procedures primarily against intensive cattle operations. VMO targeted smaller, more vulnerable operations where action would more likely yield success [49]. Stock breeders considered the overwhelming volume of objections to be a form of blackmail and accused van der Graaf of abusing the legal system. Van der Graaf received a number of threats from the cattle breeding industry [42].

Compared to Copeland, Amir and van der Graaf, Theodore Kaczynski and Franz Fuchs were less directly influenced by existing movements, though Kaczynski's views appear to have been shaped in part by Harvard University's counterculture of the 1950s and 1960s [35, 50]. Kaczynski claimed that already during his high school years he had uncomfortable fantasies of violent revenge. In his journal he writes that during high school and college he would often become terribly angry, but could not express that anger openly because he was "too strongly conditioned... against any defiance of authority" [36]. While studying at Harvard he began to recognize and formulate his feelings of loathing toward his personal situation and his anger toward society [37].

As noted earlier, university was also a significant environment in the radicalization of Amir's and van der Graaf's personalized ideologies. Referring to terrorism in general, Taylor [43, p. 127] asserts that "universities certainly have proved to be ideological training grounds for many terrorists", with the experience of university giving rise to the questioning of society's values. As we have seen, universities can also afford opportunities to directly engage with affiliated ideological milieus. However, university life does not seem to have had this effect on Franz Fuchs, whose worldview appears to have evolved largely autonomously and mainly without any direct contact with like-minded others [26].

Radicalization: The Internet and Self-Study

Communities of support for extremist beliefs and terrorist activity may be developed through virtual encounters using new social media. Recent research examines the role of the Internet as an incubator or accelerator of solo actor and small group terrorism [51, 52]. Pantucci [25, p. 34] points out that the Internet provides individuals with "direct access to a community of like-minded individuals around the world with whom they can connect and in some cases can provide them with further instigation and direction to carry out activities". For those individuals who demonstrate some level of social alienation, the community provided by the Internet "can act as a replacement social environment that they are unable to locate in the real world around them". Pantucci [25, p. 34] concludes that the Internet makes it "much easier for any alienated loner to make contact or locate a high level of both radical material, and operational support material". It should be noted, however, that the quality of this operational support material, especially online bomb-making manuals, varies considerably (e.g. [53]).

In Chap. 1, I discussed law enforcement agencies' concern that the Internet enables individuals to be radicalized in their own lounge rooms through reading, communicating extremist messages, and developing terrorist skills and expertise. The 22 July 2011 attacks in Norway illustrate this point. The accused perpetrator, Anders Breivik, was active on Internet fora and websites. He had built up substantial online connections and seems to have had a significant Facebook network; in his manifesto, Breivik [54, p. 4] speaks of "7,000 patriotic Facebook friends".[8] Breivik sent his 1,517-page manifesto to a variety of mailing lists and posted a 12-minute video on the Internet summarizing his arguments. Breivik closely followed the online statements and blogs of a number of right-wing thinkers and later cited them in his own manifesto. He also attempted to meet with at least one of these right-wing bloggers in order to discuss their ideas and beliefs [55, 56]. Breivik's online activity has reinvigorated the debate on whether lone wolves might radicalize more easily and might be more aware of like-minded others because of increased access to information, even though most of the right-wing bloggers he interacted with have explicitly distanced themselves from his actions. One newspaper goes as far as to assert that "the Internet is full of Breiviks" [57].

The case of David Copeland further illustrates the potential role of the Internet in vicariously engaging with communities of support. Copeland read right-wing texts online and learnt his bomb-making techniques through downloading and studying *The Terrorist Handbook* and *How to Make Bombs: Book Two* after visiting an Internet café [58]. Similar to the public response to the attacks in Norway, after Copeland's arrest the co-editor of the anti-fascist magazine *Searchlight* asserted that "there are many more potential Copelands in society" and called for a crackdown on the publication of inciteful and racist literature on the Internet [59].

Vicarious engagement with communities of support is clearly not restricted to the Internet. David Copeland, for instance, closely followed the media coverage of the explosion at Centennial Park during the 1996 Atlanta Olympic Games. As he watched news reports from the scene, Copeland reportedly wondered why nobody had bombed the Notting Hill Carnival. He stated that he gradually became fixated on the idea of carrying out his own bombing and "woke up one day and decided to do it" [60]. Copeland explained: "I had a thought once. It was that Centennial Park bombing. The Notting Hill Carnival was on at the same time, and I just thought why, why, why can't someone blow that place up? That'd be a good'un, you know, that would piss everyone off" [61].

The case of David Copeland points to the important role that self-study often plays in shaping the lone wolf terrorist's personalized ideology. The easy availability of extremist material both online and offline means that individuals can teach themselves the extremist creed and use this material to define and justify their actions and worldview [25]. Indeed, in some cases lone wolf terrorists bear many characteristics of an autodidactic, self-taught person. American anti-abortion activist Paul Ross Evans [79], who in 2007 attempted to bomb an abortion clinic in Austin, Texas, writes how "days were spent at the local library reading

[8] Two months after the 22 July 2011 attacks, there are numerous anti-Breivik Facebook pages that are visited and/or "liked" by tens of thousands of people, for example the page "We Hate You Anders Behring Breivik".

countless books and accessing the Internet. There is a lot of knowledge out there, just floating around, and if you are courageous enough to obtain it, you can possess the might to torment those who are your enemies". Evans [79] describes his vigorous learning activities as follows:

> As I began to contemplate taking action, I had a lot of free time on my hands.... During this period of intense research I was driven by a great inquisitiveness. I encountered numerous organizations which either directly threatened the future of Christendom, or violently killed innocent children. I grouped these various organizations into categories, and began to realistically contemplate targeting one or several of them with terrorism. I began to be consumed with an overwhelming motivation to attack specific entities with mail bombs.

In Evans' apartment police reportedly found several books, including *Pipe and Fire Bomb Designs*, *Special Forces Demolition Techniques* and William Pierce's *The Turner Diaries* [62].

David Copeland also engaged in vigorous self-study. He read racist and anti-Semitic literature, including Pierce's *The Turner Diaries* (written in 1978 under the pseudonym Andrew Macdonald [80]), and later confessed that this book was important to the construction of his worldview. Similarly, Yigal Amir immersed himself in Israel's maturing right-wing counterculture. Amir avidly read the book *Baruch Hagever* (Baruch, the Man), written and published by Baruch Goldstein admirers [40]. Most of the essays in *Baruch Hagever* address the Jewish-Muslim conflict with a Goldstein-like interpretation of what should be done in a time of unfolding crisis. One essay in the book, written by Benjamin Ze'ev Kahane, the son of the slain rabbi Meir Kahane and the influential young leader of Kahane Chai, also discusses the failure of the Jews to display determination towards the Palestinians. Kahane emphasizes that a cultural war between the real and Hellenized Jews is forcefully being waged, with the secular Hellenized Jews on the winning side. He identifies the delicate passage between targeting Arabs, which was the "virtue" of Goldstein, and targeting Jews, so tragically expressed by Amir [63, p. 113]. Amir later spoke about Rabin's cultural war against the real Jews [64].

Volkert van der Graaf, on the other hand, studied a range of anarchistic literature including books such as *Resistance is Possible: Handbook for Activists*, *The Anarchist Cookbook*, *Handbook Against the Copper*, and *Interrogation Methods*. Finally, Theodore Kaczynski was an avid reader of Joseph Conrad's novels, especially his 1907 book *The Secret Agent* [81]. Kaczynski's targeting of scientists and technological experts and his condemnation of science were reportedly inspired by the novel [65]. Like the bomb-builder in the novel, who is known as "the Professor", Kaczynski had given up a university position to live as a recluse. Kaczynski seems to have used "Conrad" or "Konrad" as an alias on at least three occasions [65]. He confessed that he grew up with a copy of the book and that he read it more than a dozen times. Kaczynski apparently failed to see that Conrad's novels are "ferocious satires of the revolutionary mind-set" [66]. For this reason, Teachout [66] argues that the Unabomber's manifesto is the work of "a mind floating in a cultural vacuum".

6.4 Lone Wolf Terrorism and Inversion

The characterization of Kaczynski's manifesto as the work of "a mind floating in a cultural vacuum" [66] directs our attention to the process of inversion which, as discussed earlier, is central to Michel Wieviorka's [16] theory of terrorism. Wieviorka [16, p. 10] notes that terrorism is:

> unique inasmuch as it is possessed of a dual specificity: on the one hand, it necessarily associates ideology with practice, and its self-image with the bearing of arms; on the other, it is perpetrated by groups which are always relatively external to the movement of which it is the inverted image.

May lone wolf terrorism be so viewed? Although at first glance the focus in Wieviorka's theory on group-actor terrorism seems to invalidate this theory for explaining lone wolf terrorism, I have shown how lone wolf terrorists are more often than not strongly influenced by broader communities of belief. Thus, it becomes possible to explore whether lone wolf terrorists can be viewed as the "inverted image" of the communities in whose name they claim to fight.

In relation to the principle of identity, the key question is whether lone wolf terrorists speak on behalf of any real social entity, as opposed to some mythic or abstract entity or belief. The accused Norwegian lone wolf Anders Behring Breivik is a case in point. As noted in Chap. 4, Breivik's personalized ideology appears to have been strongly inspired by a right-wing intellectual current referred to as counterjihad [67]. In his manifesto, Breivik [54, pp. 388, 610] makes himself out to be the embodied consciousness of all "ethnic Europeans" whose societies are under "the imminent threat of the dark force that is trying to undermine all things civil we believe in". By relying on terrorism to transmit his message that resumes some of the key meanings conveyed by the right-wing currents that oppose the "Islamization" of the West, Breivik gives a distorted image of them—an inversion. Most counterjihad and right-wing thinkers cited in his manifesto have strongly condemned Breivik's actions. Siv Jensen, the leader of Norway's Progress Party, of which Breivik was once a member, described the attacks as "horrible and cowardly". Jensen stated: "The horrible and cowardly attacks we've witnessed are contrary to the principles and values underpinning the Norwegian society. It makes me feel extra sad to know that this person once was a member of our party" [68]. The Dutch right-wing politician Geert Wilders, who is cited several times in the manifesto, stated that his Freedom Party (PVV) "abhors all that Breivik represents and has done". He said that all of those killed or injured had been "innocent victims", and reportedly described the perpetrator as "a violent and sick character" [69]. In response to accusations that his rhetoric and ideas could be stimulating and a breeding ground for radicals such as Breivik (e.g. [70]), Wilders stressed that "in no possible way have I contributed to a climate in which murderers such as Anders Breivik feel called upon to the urge to use violence" [71]. Wilders went on to state:

> The Freedom Party has never, ever called for violence and will never do. We believe in the power of the ballot box and the wisdom of the voter. Not bombs and guns. We fight for a

> democratic and nonviolent means against the further Islamisation of society and will continue to do so. The preservation of our freedom and security is our only goal [82].

However, even in the wake of the Norwegian tragedy Wilders refused to shun controversial statements regarding the threat of Islam: "I speak the truth concerning Islam and the enormous dangers of this violent totalitarian ideology. ... Truth is that the Islamization of the Netherlands must be stopped. That is not inciting hatred ... but standing up for the Netherlands and our own culture and freedom, where Islam does not belong" [71].

The case of Yigal Amir is also indicative of the inversion of the principle of identity. Amir believed that he had a moral duty and a religious commandment to kill the Israeli Prime Minister. However, the vast majority of the organizations and individuals with whom he identified and who spoke the language of delegitimation did not really wish to see Rabin dead, and even the most radical activists were probably not mentally ready to murder him [40]. Amir has always denied that ultranationalist rabbinical authorities had approved the murder of Rabin, insisting that he had decided on the killing alone after careful deliberation:

> If you knew me, I'm an individualist, I always was. I don't feel influenced, I never felt influenced. I think about everything a very great deal, like my faith and like what I did with Rabin. What I did with Rabin was done after a great, great deal of thought and after many, many other attempts I had made to awaken the nation here [72].

Amir told investigators that he had discussed the issue with several rabbis, but none of them were willing to approve the assassination arguing that it is forbidden to murder a Jew, and certainly the Prime Minister. Amir was disappointed with the rabbis, accusing them of being "soft and political" [72]. He stated that he admired no prominent rabbi in this generation. Amir believed he was fully cognizant of the relevant Jewish religious law and had a sufficient understanding of the misery of the Israeli people to act on his own [40, 73].

With regard to the principle of opposition, we have seen how the lone wolf terrorist's vilification or demonization of the enemy can drive an impetus for violent action to defend the aggrieved or remedy the perceived injustice. Wieviorka [16, p. 294] notes that "by objectivizing his enemies, and viewing himself as the hero in a resistance movement carried out in the name of values and principles which he alone is capable of justifying ... the terrorist actor exits the political arena with no thought of ever returning". Indeed, all of the lone wolf terrorists in the five case studies felt that they had exhausted all other political means or that such means would be fruitless. In their view, violence was the only way to defeat their enemies and take the blinders off their audiences. As Amir states: "I tried to do everything else, but the Government's method here is to silence demonstrations" [72]. In a similar vein, Kaczynski [74, p. 16] writes that "in order to get our message before the public with some chance of making a lasting impression, we've had to kill people". Furthermore, reflecting on his third bombing attack, David Copeland told police: "I didn't feel joy but I didn't feel sadness. I just didn't feel anything. I just had to do it. It was my destiny" [75]. Similarly, during his trial Volkert van der Graaf stated that he had killed Fortuyn "guided by my conscience". He argued that although "normally, I find it morally reprehensible to kill someone", at the time he felt it was "justified" [76]. In van der Graaf's mind, his victim was "an ever-increasing danger to society that had to be stopped [77]. Finally, the accused Norwegian terrorist Anders Breivik believes that his attacks were "atrocious but necessary" [78]. Breivik [54, p. 1396] states that he had come to the conclusion that "it would be impossible to change the system democratically".

In sum, the above suggests that lone wolf terrorists typically feel that they have the moral authority to counter-attack the morally corrupt force (the enemy) that contradicts their ideology, often regardless of the collateral damage inflicted as long as the "greater good" is achieved [37]. Lone wolf terrorists tend to believe that they are important (if not crucial) to the struggle, and that their actions will help to enlighten their audiences. We see here an aggravated subjectivism in which the lone wolf terrorist defines himself or herself through a total commitment to the cause for which he or she is the self-proclaimed vanguard and the embodied consciousness of all who have been alienated or are under threat. However, I should note here that the degree to which lone wolf terrorists consider collateral damage as morally justified tends to vary. Consider for example anti-abortion activist Paul Ross Evans' [79] confession that even though he set out "to kill those targeted", he was "determined to keep any collateral damage to a bare minimum" and therefore chose his targets "scrupulously". Evans [79] writes:

> As I compiled a list of potential targets, I focused only on those having addresses such that minimum numbers of non-targeted individuals, especially children, would be anywhere nearby. Targets who stood out from the rest and seemed to beg for retribution were those who generated disgrace toward the morally upright, and those who operated with flamboyance, arrogance, and smugness.

The target selection and modus operandi of lone wolf terrorists are the focus of Chap. 7.

References

1. Senate of the United States (2007) Violent radicalization and homegrown terrorism prevention act of 2007. US Senate, Washington. http://frwebgate.access.gpo.gov/cgi-bin/getdoc.cgi?dbname=110_cong_bills&docid=f:h1955rfs.txt.pdf. Accessed 22 September 2011
2. Reinares F, Alonso R, Bjørgo T, Della Porta D, Coolsaet R, Khosrokhavar F, Lohlker R, Ranstorp M, Schmid A, Silke A, Taarnby M, de Vries G (2008) Radicalisation processes leading to acts of terrorism. European Commission Expert Group on Violent Radicalisation, Brussels
3. Turk A (2008) Sociology of terrorism. In: Matson R (ed) The spirit of sociology: a reader. Pearson, Boston, pp 490–502
4. Hudson R (1999) The sociology and psychology of terrorism: Who becomes a terrorist and why?. Federal Research Division, Library of Congress, Washington
5. Borum R (2004) Psychology of terrorism. University of South Florida, Tampa
6. Moghaddam F (2005) The staircase to terrorism: a psychological exploration. Am Psychol 60(2):161–169

7. Bjørgo T (ed) (2005) Root causes of terrorism: Myths, reality and way forward. Routledge, London
8. Silber M, Bhatt A (2007) Radicalization in the West: the homegrown threat. NYPD, New York
9. Slootman M, Tillie J (2006) Processen van radicalisering: Waarom sommige Amsterdamse moslims radicaal worden. IMES, Universiteit van Amsterdam, Amsterdam
10. Dalgaard-Nielsen A (2008) Studying violent radicalisation in Europe: the potential contribution of social-psychological and psychological approaches. Danish Institute for International Studies, Copenhagen
11. Dalgaard-Nielsen A (2010) Violent radicalization in Europe: what we know and what we do not know. Stud Confl Terror 33(9):797–814
12. McCauley C, Moskalenko S (2008) Mechanisms of political radicalization: pathways toward terrorism. Terror Politi Violence 20(3):415–433
13. TTSRL (2008) Radicalisation, recruitment and the EU counter-radicalisation strategy. European Commission Sixth Framework program Transnational Terrorism, Security and the Rule of Law, Brussels
14. van der Pligt J, Koomen W (2009) Achtergronden en determinanten van radicalisering en terrorisme. Universiteit van Amsterdam/WODC, Amsterdam
15. Della Porta D (1995) Social movements, political violence and the state. Cambridge University Press, Cambridge
16. Wieviorka M (2003) The making of terrorism, 2nd edn. University of Chicago Press, Chicago
17. Horgan J, Taylor M (2001) The making of a terrorist. Jane's Intell Rev 13(12):16–18
18. Spaaij R (2010) The enigma of lone wolf terrorism: an assessment. Stud Confl Terror 33(9):854–870
19. Jackson P (2011) Solo actor terrorism and the mythology of the lone wolf. In: Gable G, Jackson P (eds) Lone wolves: Myth or reality?. Searchlight, Ilford, pp 79–88
20. Borum R (2012) Psychology of terrorism. In: Christie DJ (ed) Encyclopedia of peace psychology. Wiley-Blackwell, Malden
21. Post JM (1998) Terrorist psycho-logic: terrorist behavior as a product of psychological forces. In: Reich W (ed) Origins of terrorism. Woodrow Wilson Center Press, Washington, pp 25–41
22. Horgan J (2005) The psychology of terrorism. Routledge, London
23. Crenshaw M (2003) The causes of terrorism. In: Kegley CW Jr (ed) The new global terrorism: characteristics, Causes, controls. Prentice Hall, Upper Saddle River, pp 92–105
24. Hewitt C (2003) Understanding terrorism in America: from the Klan to al Qaeda. Routledge, New York
25. Pantucci R (2011) A typology of lone wolves: preliminary analysis of lone Islamist terrorists. ICSR, London
26. Spaaij R (2007) Lone-wolf terrorism. In: Report for the European commission sixth framework program transnational terrorism, security and the rule of law. COT Institute for Safety, Security and Crisis Management, The Hague
27. Turchie T, Puckett K (2007) Hunting the American terrorist: The FBI's war on homegrown terror. History Publishing Company, Palisades
28. Borum R (2011) Lone wolf terrorism. In: Martin CG (ed) The SAGE encyclopedia of terrorism, 2nd edn. Sage, London, pp 361–362
29. Public Prosecution of the Netherlands (2003) Closing speech public prosecutor, 1 April. http://www.om.nl/dossier/de_zaak_fortuyn/_de_zaak_fortuyn_nieuwsberichten/21709/. Accessed 3 May 2007
30. Netherlands Broadcasting Foundation (NOS) (2003) Achttien jaar cel voor Volkert van der G. http://nos.nl/archief/2004/nieuws/index.html#@http://nos.nl/archief/2004/nieuws/dossiers/pim_fortuyn/2003/maart/2603_voorbeschouwing_proces.htm. Accessed 14 June 2007
31. Friedrichsen G (1999) Nur irgendein Kasperl?. Der Spiegel, 22 February, 184–186
32. Böhmer R (2002) Der Briefbomber von Österreich: Eine anankastische Persönlichkeit. GRIN Verlag, Munich

33. Buncombe A (2000) Nail bomber is 'bad in the old-fashioned way, not ill'. The Independent, 29 June
34. Clough S (2000) Bomber 'yearned to be a mass killer'. The Daily Telegraph, 19 June
35. Chase A (2003) Harvard and the Unabomber: the education of an American terrorist. W.W. Norton, New York
36. Johnson SC (1998) Psychological evaluation of Theodore John Kaczynski. Federal Correctional Institution Butner, North Carolina
37. Springer N (2009) Patterns of radicalization: Identifying the markers and warning signs of domestic lone wolf terrorists in our midst. Unpublished Master's thesis, Naval Postgraduate School, Monterey.
38. Müller T (2006) Beestmensen: Vermomming, leugens en strategie van seriemoordenaars. Mets and Schilt, Amsterdam
39. BBC (2000) Profile: copeland the killer. BBC News, 30 June
40. Sprinzak E (1999) Brother against brother: violence and extremism in Israeli politics from Altalena to the Rabin assassination. The Free Press, New York
41. Kifner J (1995) Belief to blood: the making of Rabin's killer. The New York Times, 19 Nov
42. de Jong S, Niemöller J (2003a) Volkert's verborgen verleden. HP/De Tijd, 4 July, pp 26–36
43. Taylor M (1988) The terrorist. Brassey's Defence Publishers, London
44. Juergensmeyer M (2000) Terror in the mind of God: the global rise of religious violence. University of California Press, Berkeley
45. Mullins S (2009) Parallels between crime and terrorism: a social psychological perspective. Stud Confl Terror 32(9):811–830
46. Clough S (2000) Nail bomber tried to start 'a race war'. The Daily Telegraph, 6 June
47. Lewis A (1995) On God's orders. The New York Times, 6 Nov
48. Siebelt P (2003) Eco nostra: het netwerk achter Volkert van der Graaf. Aspekt, Soesterberg
49. Parker JL (2005) Jihad vegan. New Criminologist, 20 June. http://newcriminologist.co.uk/news.asp?id=206663208. Accessed 8 May 2007
50. Chase A (2004) A mind for murder: The education of the Unabomber and the origins of modern terrorism. W.W. Norton, New York
51. Sageman M (2008) Leaderless jihad: terror networks in the twenty-first century. University of Pennsylvania Press, Philadelphia
52. Weimann G (2006) Terror on the internet. United States Institute of Peace Press, Washington
53. Cruickshank P, Lister T (2011) The 'lone wolf'—The unknowable terror. CNN Security Clearance Blog, 7 Sept. http://security.blogs.cnn.com/2011/09/07/the-lone-wolf-the-unknowable-face-of-terror/. Accessed 9 September 2011
54. Breivik A (2011) 2083: a European declaration of independence. http://www.washingtonpost.com/r/2010-2019/WashingtonPost/2011/07/24/National-Politics/Graphics/2083+-+A+European+Declaration+of+Independence.pdf. Accessed 26 July 2011
55. Hopperstad M (2011) Breivik's political idol 'Fjordman' emerges from anonymity. Verdengs Gang, 5 Aug. http://www.vg.no/nyheter/innenriks/oslobomben/artikkel.php?artid=10089390
56. Klis H (2011) Terrorist Breivik haalde deze man 111 keer aan in zijn manifest. NRC.nl, 5 Aug. http://www.nrc.nl/nieuws/2011/08/05/terrorist-breivik-haalde-deze-man-111-keer-aan-in-zijn-manifest/
57. de Jong S (2011) Op Internet wemelt het van de 'Breiviks'. Profeet Wilders moet geweldsretoriek uitleggen. NRC.nl, 26 July. http://www.nrc.nl/nieuws/2011/07/26/op-internet-wemelt-het-van-de-breiviks-profeet-wilders-moet-geweldsretoriek-uitleggen/. Accessed 28 July
58. Clough S (2000) Bombings 'inspired by Atlanta attack'. The Daily Telegraph, 6 June
59. Hopkins N (2000) Bomber gets six life terms: Copeland driven by virulent hatred and pitiless contempt, says judge. The Guardian, 1 July
60. Bennetto J (2000) Police took just 14 days to track down nail bomber. The Independent, 30 June

61. BBC (2000) Transcript of BBC Panorama: The nailbomber. Recorded from transmission BBC1, 30 June. London: BBC. http://news.bbc.co.uk/hi/english/static/audio_video/programmes/panorama/transcripts/transcript_30_06_00.txt. Accessed 10 June 2007
62. Anti-Defamation League (2007) Texas abortion clinic bomber admits to other mail bombs. 10 Aug. http://www.adl.org/learn/extremism_in_the_news/Other_Extremism/abortion+bomb+7.07.htm?LEARN_Cat=Extremism&LEARN_SubCat=Extremism_in_the_News. Accessed 12 August 2011
63. Sprinzak E (2000) Israel's radical right and the countdown to the Rabin assassination. In: Peri Y (ed) The assassination of Yitzhak Rabin. Stanford University Press, Stanford, pp 96–128
64. Karpin M, Friedman I (1998) Murder in the name of God: the plot to kill Yitzhak Rabin. Henry Holt and Co, New York
65. Associated Press (1996) Joseph Conrad novel may have influenced alleged Unabomber. The Spokesman-Review, 9 July
66. Teachout T (1996) Mad loner builds perfect bomb. The New York Times, 13 July
67. Hegghammer T (2011) The rise of the macro-nationalists. The New York Times, 30 July. Accessed 3 August 2011
68. Ames P (2011) Is Anders Behring Breivik part of a movement? Global Post, 25 July. http://www.globalpost.com/dispatch/news/regions/europe/110724/europe-right-wing-political-parties-Breivik-manifesto. Accessed 26 August 2011
69. Cluskey P (2011) Wilders describes suspect as 'violent and sick'. The Irish Times, 25 July
70. von der Dunk T (2011) Breivik trok logische consequentie uit Wilders' retoriek. De Volkskrant, 5 Sept
71. Mikkers R (2011) Wilders woest om 'hetze' na Noors drama. De Telegraaf, 1 Aug
72. Greenberg J (1995) Rabin killer denies rabbi approved act. The New York Times, 1 Dec
73. Greenberg J (1995) Israeli police question 2 rabbis in Rabin assassination. The New York Times, 27 Nov
74. Kaczynski T (1995) Industrial society and its future (Unabomber's Manifesto). http://www.provokateur.com/webres/Unabomber%20Manifesto%20by%20Theodore%20Kaczynski. Accessed 8 June 2007
75. Buncombe A (2000) 'Inspiration' came from Atlanta Olympics bomb. The Independent, 30 June
76. Sage A (2003) Pim Fortuyn's killer is jailed for 18 years. The Times, 16 April
77. ANP (Netherlands National News Agency) (2002) Volkert van der G. bekent moord op Pim Fortuyn. De Volkskrant, 23 Nov
78. Boyes R, Barraclough A (2011) Slaughter cruel but necessary, says gunman Anders Breivik. The Australian, 25 July
79. Evans PR (n.d.) Methodical terrorism: How and why. http://www.armyofgod.com/POCPaulRossEvansMethodicalTerrorism.html. Accessed 12 August 2011
80. Macdonald A (1978) The Turner Diaries. Hillsboro, WV: National Vanguard Books
81. Conrad J (1907) The Secret Agent. London: J. M. Dent & Co
82. Wilders G (2011) Statement by Geert Wilders concerning the Norway massacre. LiveLeak.com, 26 July. http://www.liveleak.com/view?i=0a7_1311673966. Accessed 29 July 2011

Chapter 7
Modus Operandi

7.1 Planning for Terror

> Never rush into anything, time and planning are keys to success.
> - White supremacist Tom Metzger [1].

In the aftermath of the double terrorist attack in Norway on 22 July 2011, it became apparent that the alleged perpetrator, Anders Behring Breivik, had meticulously planned the attacks. Breivik's copious writings suggest that he planned his operations at least months in advance, gradually gathering the tools and the expertise he needed to carry out the attacks. Breivik [2] describes a long preparation phase during which he writes, reads, attends shooting classes, buys weapons, chemicals and other supplies, studies online bomb-making manuals, and spends the last 80 days manufacturing the explosive devices. Breivik [2, p. 1470] writes that it would have taken him only 30 days had he had experience:

> If I had known then, what I know today, by following this guide, I would have managed to complete the operation within 30 days instead of using almost 80 days. By following my guide, anyone can create the foundation for a spectacular operation with only one person in less than a month even if adding two "resting" days!

Breivik seems to have begun his preparations in earnest in April 2011, when he rented a farm in the village of Aasta, several hours drive from Oslo. His stated intention was to grow sugar beets because he had learned that they require a large amount of fertilizer, which he planned to use to make bombs [3]. Breivik [2, p. 1454] writes:

> I made the order for the fertilizer which were [*sic*] to be delivered a week later. Prior to making this order I had officially registered my company as an agricultural entity, with emphasis on the growing of specific crops, and I had gotten my official production number (a farming number) allowing me to make orders from the national farming supplier. If they were to screen me they would see that my company was linked to a farm that had 90 decares of fertile land so all was well.

The six tons of fertilizer he ordered were delivered to his farm on 4 May. By that time, Breivik had rented the first of two vehicles he used in the attacks; in mid-June,

R. Spaaij, *Understanding Lone Wolf Terrorism*, SpringerBriefs in Criminology, DOI: 10.1007/978-94-007-2981-0_7, © The Author(s) 2012

he rented the second vehicle, a larger van. The task Breivik set for himself was to mix the ingredients for the explosives in the privacy of the farm [3].

In the minutely detailed diary he began compiling in the months leading up to the attacks, Breivik describes how he assembled the explosives he would use in the Oslo car bomb. He also discusses how he prepared for the shooting spree he would then launch on the island of Utøya. Breivik owned a Glock semi-automatic pistol and a .223 Ruger Mini-14 rifle [4]. Initially, Breivik [2, p. 1465], writes, he bought hollow-point bullets, but he later replaced them with soft-point bullets which he deemed "more suitable for the purpose of inflicting maximum damage to vermin". After his arrest, Breivik reportedly confessed that he had considered other possible government and Labour Party targets to strike [5]. He bought a police uniform which he used to disguise himself as a police officer on the island of Utøya on the day of the attack. In order to support fellow crusaders, Breivik also writes in detail about the mistakes he made. He argues: "Learning from other peoples [*sic*] mistakes is always preferable to making them all yourself. It should be possible to drastically reduce the time spent on preparation, assembly and manufacturing based on the experiences shared in this log" [2, p. 1454].

By 22 July, the day of the attacks, he had driven the two vehicles to Oslo. One of the vehicles may have been carrying more than 1,000 pounds of explosives [3]. From his writings it appears that Breivik had apparently made no getaway plans, nor did he choose to give up his own life in the cause of his crusade. On the morning of the attacks, he wrote his final entry into his diary: "Initiate blasting sequences at pre-determined sites. ... I believe this will be my last entry. It is now Fri July 22nd, 12.51" [2, pp. 1470–1471]. Less than three hours later the car bomb was detonated.

There is still much that we do not know about the attacks, and Breivik's own account of his preparations for the attacks seems to be inaccurate or exaggerated, at least in places. For example, in his manifesto Breivik [2, p. 4] claims that he spent in "excess of 300,000 Euros" on the operation, and he subsequently told police that he used more than double that amount [6]. We can therefore not be sure that Breivik's writings are reliable, and it seems that he has lied in court on at least a number of occasions. Overall, however, Breivik's diary appears to provide a chilling and "largely plausible picture" of the mundane details he attended to as he prepared for his attacks [3].

From what we know about lone wolf terrorism, it is clear that Breivik's meticulous planning is by no means unique. Lone wolf terrorists typically plan and prepare their attacks carefully and thoroughly, albeit to a variable degree and with varying success. Anti-abortion activist Paul Ross Evans, who was cited at length in the previous chapter, is a case in point. In his essay "Methodical Terrorism", Evans [39] gives a detailed description of his modus operandi. He writes how he became consumed with an "overwhelming motivation" to attack specific targets with bombs. Evans believed that he could "operate for long periods of time, gain some ground, and generally aggravate adversaries, all the while avoiding detection". His stated intention was "to generate media attention toward Christianity's dissatisfaction with the offending parties" and "to coerce the government of the

United States to renounce its present agenda", among other things. As noted in Chap. 6, Evans appears to have carefully chosen his targets, who he intended to kill, in order to "keep any collateral damage to a bare minimum" [39].

Evans further explains that he possessed very little knowledge about the manufacture and detonation of improvised explosive devices, but that he did have a basic understanding of chemistry and had even created some small explosive devices as an adolescent. Evans [39] writes that he had "little or no money, and lacked the resources necessary to obtain high-explosive materials". He reportedly made several purchases at local hardware and retail grocery stores, researched the Internet and experimented with various items. Evans confesses: "The conviction to act out against The Enemy was overpowering. The truth of the matter is that I loved this work. My times of bomb making were to me times when I felt that I was doing what I had been born to do—to be a thorn in the side of the Evil One" [39]. Despite his strong conviction, Evans' attack on the Austin Women's Health Center, on 25 April 2007, failed. Evans placed the homemade bomb, which contained some 2,000 nails, in the parking lot near the clinic entrance and activated the timer. However, the bomb did not detonate because the triggering wire did not make contact with the explosive material. A bomb squad disposed of the device after receiving a call about a suspicious package. There were no injuries [7].

Beyond these personal accounts of how specific lone wolf terrorist attacks were planned and carried out, the database (see Appendix) affords a more general overview of the modi operandi of lone wolf terrorists, especially with regard to the selection of targets and weapons. Let us first consider the targets of lone wolf terrorism.

7.2 Targets

Figure 7.1 categorizes the targets attacked by the lone wolf terrorists in the database. The figure shows that lone wolf terrorists principally target civilians (58%), which broadly reflects the targets of terrorist incidents in general [8]. Some definitions of terrorism specifically include the targeting of civilians or noncombatants as a key normative principle distinguishing terrorism from other forms of polical violence. Ganor [9, p. 288], for instance, argues that "even if its declared ultimate goals are legitimate, an organization that deliberately targets civilians is a terrorist organization". Government officials and politicians (13%), and health practitioners (10%), are the second and third most frequently targeted categories. In all nine cases in which lone wolf terrorists targeted health practitioners, the victims were medical staff working in abortion provision clinics; eight of these cases took place in the United States. This geographical concentration of lone wolf terrorist attacks targeting health practitioners can be explained by the relative popularity of the leaderless resistance strategy among radical anti-abortion activists in the United States whose principal targets are medical doctors who perform or support abortions.

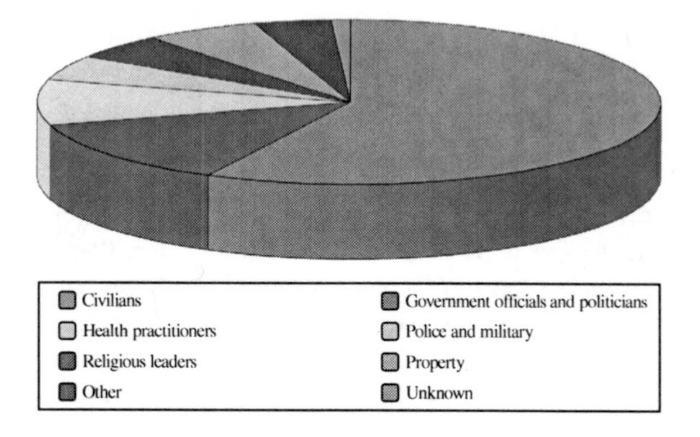

Fig. 7.1 Targets of lone wolf terrorism (Some lone wolf terrorists have attacked multiple targets, all of which have been accounted for in Fig. 7.1)

The case studies provide detailed insight into how lone wolf terrorists select their targets, showing that they typically attack symbolic targets. Where the lone wolf terrorist carries out a series of attacks (as opposed to a single attack), he or she may choose a range of targets which are seen as being of symbolic significance and discursively fit into the category of "the enemy". Indeed, symbolism is a key feature of terrorism and the symbol in an act of terrorism is often communicated in the specific target of the terrorist attack [40]. Terrorism is symbolic in that it is "intended to illustrate or refer to something beyond the immediate target", for instance a grander, less tangible goal or conquest [10, p. 123]. Most terrorist targets at some level symbolize the perceived righteousness of the particular terrorist's cause and the perceived evil of the opponent he or she is fighting. Symbolism can be used to rationalize acts of mass violence and can be manipulated to fit any number of targets into the (often loosely defined) category of "the enemy" [11].

Three of the five lone wolf terrorists in the case studies targeted civilians, whilst the other two (Yigal Amir and Volkert van der Graaf) targeted politicians. Franz Fuchs and Theodore Kaczynski targeted a variety of categories; the former attacked civilians, journalists, religious leaders, government officials and health practitioners, while the latter attacked scientists, business people and civilians. The cases of Yigal Amir and Franz Fuchs illustrate how targets come to be seen as symbolic of a perceived evil. By assassinating Rabin, Amir tried to make a difference—if not in a direct, strategic sense of changing the political order in Israel and to "save" the land and the nation, then in an indirect way as a dramatic performance so powerful as to change people's perceptions of the world [10]. For Amir, the assassination of Rabin was an exemplary act that symbolized the fight against an illegitimate government that was prepared to cede Jewish holy land to the Palestinians [12]. He told investigators that the biblical heritage of the Jews was under imminent threat and that the media ignored the protests of the Israeli far right. Had these protests been properly covered in the mass media, Amir argued, he might not have assassinated the Prime Minister [13].

Whereas Yigal Amir carried out a single attack on the Israeli Prime Minister, Franz Fuchs' terrorism campaign spanned nearly three years and targeted a wide range of people. Fuchs, who had detailed knowledge of electronics, physics and chemistry, used a total of 28 improvised explosive devices in five series of bomb attacks between 1993 and 1996. All his bombs were manufactured with great precision and skill [14]. He stated that he took to heart "the increased discrimination of German Austrians and the growing self-consciousness of other ethnic groups and religions" [15]. Fuchs increasingly projected his personal frustrations and resentment on to minority ethnic groups and what he regarded and loosely defined as their representatives [14]. The first bombs were planted on 3 December 1993. The priest August Janisch, who was injured in the blast, was presumably targeted because of his public statements that Austrians were morally obligated to help refugees from the Balkan region. An hour later Silvana Meixner, a journalist specialized in minority issues, was injured in a mail bomb explosion. Fuchs' subsequent bomb attacks targeted a variety of individuals and organizations, including a refugee and immigration lawyer, the director of a humanitarian organization, Green Party politicians, Women's Minister Johanna Dohnal, the vice-mayor of Lübeck (Germany), a bilingual school, medical doctors with an immigrant background, refugee aid workers, a television host, and the stepmother of Home Affairs Minister Caspar Einem. The most devastating bombing Fuchs carried out took place on 4 February 1995 in Oberwart. Four men, all of them residents of a nearby Roma settlement, were killed when an improvised explosive device attached to a sign that read "*Roma zurück nach Indien*" (Roma back to India) exploded [16]. Fuchs later stated that it was never his intention to kill these four people [15].

How, then, do lone wolf terrorists prepare for their attack(s) on identified targets? As noted, lone wolf terrorists typically face significant challenges when attempting to translate theory into action. One major criterion for the operations of terrorists to be successful is comprehensive preparation and planning including good prior intelligence, for example from reconnaissance and observation [8]. This task can be relatively difficult to accomplish for lone individuals who do not have a support infrastructure in place. It has been argued that lone wolf terrorists are especially vulnerable to detection during the surveillance of their (potential) targets [41]. Burton [17] asserts that conducting solo surveillance against a moving target is "one of the hardest tasks any professional surveillance operative can be tasked with, and is even more difficult for an amateur… their odd behavior and crude surveillance technique—they frequently stalk and lurk—make them easy to pick out".

Whilst all five lone wolf terrorists in the case studies carefully planned their attacks, the extent and the quality of the surveillance they conducted on their targets vary significantly. Let us use the cases of van der Graaf, Amir and Copeland as examples here. Volkert van der Graaf researched Pim Fortuyn's daily program and planned public appearances. He took notes of his findings and used the Internet to obtain maps of the Mediapark in Hilversum and the 3FM building where Fortuyn was expected to give a radio interview the next day [18]. On the day of the attack, van der Graaf carried his notes and maps in a backpack alongside his gun, the cartridges and a balaclava [19]. Van der Graaf sought to disguise himself by wearing a baseball cap and dark sunglasses and by removing his earrings. He also wore a pair of latex gloves to avoid leaving fingerprints on the gun [20]. When van der Graaf arrived at the Mediapark around 4 pm, he buried the plastic bag with his gun in case he would be searched by security staff or police. He then inspected the area before hiding in the bushes next to the 3FM building. Shortly before 6 pm, van der Graaf dug up his gun and moved in the direction of parked cars facing the entrance of the 3FM building. Fortuyn emerged from the building in the company of a number of other people and van der Graaf decided to walk towards Fortuyn, pass him and then turn and open fire. He held the gun with the plastic bag around it in order to collect the bullets, shooting Fortuyn five times from less than a 1.5 meter distance. Van der Graaf later described his approach as follows:

> I had figured out that if I would approach Fortuyn from the front, he might be able to see the attack coming. Shooting Fortuyn from behind would be the least problematic. In that case he would not be able to duck away, which could cause danger for the others present at the scene. Next to that, I did not want Fortuyn to suffer more than necessary. Shooting him from behind would make it possible to kill him instantly [19].

The assassination of Yitzhak Rabin on 4 November 1995 was also carefully planned; however, Yigal Amir had significantly more difficulty in carrying out the attack. Four times Amir tried to get within firing range of Rabin [21]. He told his interrogators that he had repeatedly set out to murder Rabin but held back at the last minute, having received a "sign from heaven" that the time was not yet right [12, 13]. In January 1995, Rabin was scheduled to attend a ceremony at Yad Vashem, the Holocaust memorial in Jerusalem. Amir went to the event, but Rabin cancelled. Three months later Amir again travelled to Jerusalem to target Rabin. Amir brought a loaded gun to Sacher Park, where Rabin was expected to attend a folk festival celebrated by Israel's Moroccan Jews, but he lost his nerve and left the site. Six months later, in September, Amir staged a third attempt to kill Rabin, making his way to a ceremony dedicating a new underpass along the main highway just north of Herzliya. However, he arrived too early and again lost his nerve [12]. During his fourth and final attempt, Amir took a bus to Tel Aviv where Rabin and Shimon Peres were scheduled to address a peace rally. He carried a gun that he had bought in 1993 after obtaining a gun license. Near the Tel Aviv City Hall, Amir moved among the large crowd that had gathered for the peace rally. After inspecting the area he waited for his targets in the parking lot. His original plan appears to have been to shoot both Rabin and Peres when they left the peace rally, but when the two walked down separately from the podium, Amir focused on Rabin, who was his primary target [22].

David Copeland, on the other hand, did not generally have good prior intelligence on his targets. Copeland planted improvised explosive devices in public locations over three successive weekends in 1999. His first attack, on 17 April 1999, targeted Brixton's Electric Avenue. Copeland had a very limited understanding of his target; in fact, he had never been to Brixton before. When he arrived in Brixton on the day of the attack he walked up and down the busy High Street for more than an hour to explore the area. He decided to plant the bomb, which was hidden inside a sports bag, at a bus stop outside a local supermarket. The bag aroused the suspicion of market traders who eventually decided to open it. Inside the bag they saw a clear plastic Tupperware box with a coloured lid which was on top of a larger cardboard box. Inside the plastic box were two square batteries and a round object suggestive of an old-fashioned alarm clock. The cardboard box was filled with nails. Concern grew that it might be a bomb. The bag was moved away from the stalls and on to some wooden pallets [23]. The bomb detonated while the police were still evacuating people [24]. Approximately 50 people were injured. Over 1,500 nails of various sizes were recovered from the scene. Copeland later confessed he planted the bomb there because he "knew that Brixton was the focal point for the Black community... I put it there to get the people, the people walking by and the people at the bus stop" [25].

Copeland had planned to detonate his second bomb the following weekend at the Brick Lane street market, in the heart of London's Bangladeshi community. But arriving on the afternoon of Saturday 24 April he found the market was to be held the following morning. Rather than return home with the bomb he was carrying in a sports bag, Copeland decided to dump it in a side-street between two vehicles [24]. Copeland later explained:

> I presumed there was going to be a market of some sort up there, but it wasn't. So then I was in two minds whether to disassemble the device and go, you know, come back Sunday. Then I just... you know, decided. I walked up Brick Lane looking for somewhere to plant it. It was about an hour to go before detonation. I didn't want to be seen planting the device, so I went down Hanbury Street. There was two big vans and I slipped in between them and walked out, they masked my escape. It was like an aborted mission you could call it [26].

The bag was discovered by a motorist, but the bomb exploded while he was on the phone to the police. Thirteen people were injured. Four days later, after extensive investigation of CCTV surveillance footage, police identified a man in Brixton who had been carrying the sports bag. The CCTV images were published in the British media as police appealed for information from the public. Copeland saw his own photograph in a newspaper [27].

On his way home from Brick Lane, Copeland travelled to Soho, the centre of London's gay community, where he identified the Admiral Duncan as a "queer pub full of men hugging each other" [28]. Copeland had planned to bomb the public house the next week, but due to the publication of his photograph he decided to bring the date forward by a day. He transported his bomb-making materials to London where he stayed in a hotel under a false name. Copeland planted the bomb inside the pub on the evening of Friday 30 April. Before the attack, Copeland sat at the bar in the pub and ordered a drink. According to eyewitnesses, Copeland seemed uneasy and kept looking at his watch and up and down the bar. A man at the bar asked Copeland whether he was waiting for someone, to which he reportedly replied that he was waiting for his boyfriend [24]. Copeland then asked where the nearest bank was and left. Customers noticed

Copeland's sports bag on the floor of the bar. The assistant manager examined the outside of the bag and inquired whether it belonged to any of the customers. He then became concerned and began to move people away from the area before returning to the bag to read the writing on it. As he was standing over the bag, the bomb exploded. The explosion killed three people and injured at least 79 others. Four people required limb amputations. Over 500 nails were recovered from the scene [28].

7.3 Weapons

The modus operandi of lone wolf terrorists exhibits a number of idiosyncrasies that present both challenges and opportunities for counterterrorism. This applies not only to the selection and surveillance of potential targets, but also to weapon selection. Depending on their level of risk aversion (or risk seeking behaviour) and their resources and capability (real or perceived), lone wolf terrorists will predominantly choose assassination, armed attack, bombing, hostage taking or unconventional attacks [29]. The database provides insight into the weapons used in lone wolf terrorism. Figure 7.2 shows that firearms and explosives are the most common weapons of attack used by lone wolf terrorists. Firearms are used by 43% of lone wolves, while explosives are utilized in 28% of cases. The armed hijacking of an aircraft or bus (16%) and arson (6%) are the third and fourth most popular weapons of choice.[9]

Lone wolf terrorists' use of firearms is significantly more prevalent in the United States, where 28 lone wolves (70%) have used firearms, than in the other countries. This dissimilarity may well be explained by the relative ease with which (semiautomatic) firearms and gun licences can be acquired in the United States compared to most of the other countries in the research sample. In contrast, armed hijackings are relatively rare in lone wolf terrorist attacks in the United States, where only one attack, in February 1983, involved the hijacking of an aircraft. Armed with a rifle and possibly an explosive device, Hussein Shey Kholya hijacked an aircraft during a one-hour flight from Killeen, Texas, en route to Dallas-Fort Worth Regional Airport. Kholya took 21 people hostage and only released them after diverting the plane to land in Nuevo Laredo, Mexico. Kholya reportedly opposed US foreign policy towards Iran and wanted to make Americans aware of the conditions in Iran.

Only one incident of lone wolf terrorism involved the (threatened) use of nuclear, biological, radiological or chemical (NBRC) weapons, which are often referred to as "weapons of mass destruction" (e.g. [30]). In 1974, Muharem Kurbegovic threatened to release sarin in populated areas and claimed that he was already conducting experiments with it. He may also have been experimenting

[9] Armed hijackings often involve the use of a firearm, knife or explosive device.

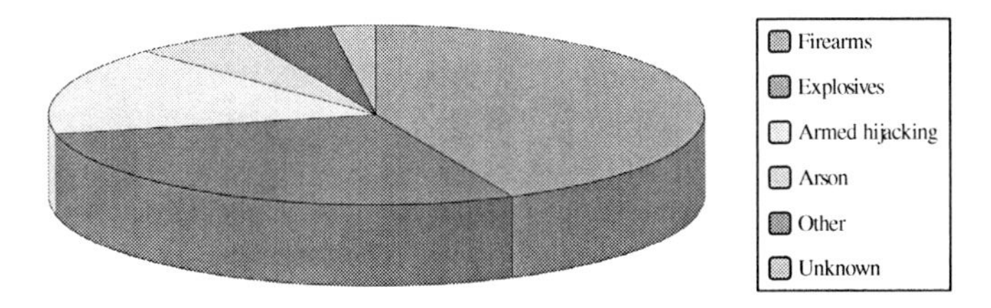

Fig. 7.2 Weapons used by lone wolf terrorists

with other chemical agents. It is known that Kurbegovic had acquired various chemicals, including a large amount of sodium cyanide [31]. Considering that this is the only recorded case of lone wolf terrorism involving unconventional weapons, that Kurbegovic did not go through with it, and that this case occurred over three decades ago, there is no empirical evidence to support Laqueur's [32] claim that lone individuals are among the most likely candidates to use weapons of mass destruction. Furthermore, given the practical difficulties associated with the manufacturing and dispersal of NBRC materials for terrorist purposes, it seems that even if lone wolf terrorists were willing and able to use such weapons, the most likely impact would be "mass disruption" rather than mass destruction [33]. However, such small-scale attacks could nonetheless instil considerable fear in the population.[10]

The data on the weapons used in lone wolf terrorist attacks are particularly interesting when compared to weapons utilized in group-actor terrorism. Whilst firearms are the most common weapon used by lone wolf terrorists, bombings and firebombings are the dominant form of terrorist incident, accounting annually for 65–75% of all international terrorist attacks [8]. Lone wolf terrorism thus partially differs from group-actor terrorism with regard to the weapons used. One main reason for this is that, as the case of Paul Ross Evans discussed earlier suggests, manufacturing a potent improvised explosive device is technically demanding, especially for a lone individual with no prior experience in bomb-making [35]. There may thus exist a disconnect between intention and capability with regard to which weapon(s) a lone wolf terrorist seeks to use.

Consider for example David Copeland, who obtained information on how to make bombs from manuals posted on the Internet. Some of the devices described in these manuals are fairly sophisticated while others are more rudimentary, involving materials that are readily available in high street shops and hardware stores. Copeland purchased sports bags, alarm clocks for timing devices, hundreds of nails and other materials he needed to make explosive devices. He also bought large quantities of fireworks for a total of up to 1,500 GBP to provide gunpowder and stole the chemicals he needed to make high explosives [24]. Copeland then

[10] The anthrax letters sent in the United States in 2001 are a case in point. One main lesson to be learned from the anthrax exposure incidents is that terrorists do not have to kill many people to create panic and foment fear and insecurity. Indeed, as Hoffman [34] notes, "five persons dying in mysterious circumstances is quite effective at unnerving an entire nation".

began experimenting with small explosives but found that he was not able to assemble the necessary ingredients as indicated in the Internet guides, probably partly because online bomb-making manuals tend to contain significant errors [36]. For this reason, Copeland instead resorted to a less sophisticated bomb made out of firework material [37]. He later stated that he finally succeeded in producing a simpler bomb that was a "plastic pipe about a foot long. It was glued at both ends. I put it in a cardboard box and covered it with nails. They'd smash into windows, stick into people, maim people and kill people" [26].

Notwithstanding the difficulties he faced in constructing his weaponry, Copeland's bomb attacks demonstrate that lone individuals can produce lethal explosives and learn and improve their bomb-making techniques over time through practice. Paul Ross Evans [39] hints at this when he writes: "I was still very much experimenting. Eventually, I would have killed people... It doesn't reflect my deficiency as a bomb maker, it just reflects what one may encounter as a lone bomb maker while learning and cultivating himself, as a process".

Theodore Kaczynski's extensive bombing campaign that spanned almost 18 years illustrates this point well. Even a highly intelligent person like Kaczynski had to do much experimentation in order to improve the design of his improvised explosive devices. Of the 16 bombs Kaczynski sent, several either did not explode or did not function as designed [35]. In the end, his 18-year bombing campaign claimed only three lives. However, the lethality of Kaczynski's explosives increased significantly over the years. His first bomb, in May 1978, targeted Professor Buckley Crist at Northwestern University. The package was found in a parking lot at the University of Illinois at Chicago and sent back to the return address at Northwestern University. It exploded at the return address, injuring a police officer who opened the package. The bomb was crudely made with plumbing pipe and electrical wire from a lamp. It contained smokeless explosive powders and the box and the plugs that sealed the pipe ends were handcrafted of wood. A more efficient technique later employed by Kaczynski was to use batteries and heat-filament wire to ignite the explosives faster and more effectively. The US authorities recognized the increasing complexity and lethality of Kaczynski's improvised explosive devices. In 1993, FBI bomb experts found that the devices "were now of such a level of complexity and sophistication that they would each have required a hundred hours of careful assembly" [38, p. 280]. In the next chapter, we shift our attention to the ways in which lone wolf terrorist attacks of this kind have been responded to.

References

1. Metzger T (n.d.) Laws for the lone wolf. http://www.resist.com/Articles/literature/LawsForTheLoneWolfByTomMetzger.htm. Accessed 15 August 2011
2. Breivik A (2011) 2083: a European declaration of independence. http://www.washingtonpost.com/r/2010-2019/WashingtonPost/2011/07/24/National-Politics/Graphics/2083+-+A+European+Declaration+of+Independence.pdf. Accessed 26 July 2011

3. Englund W (2011) In diary, Norwegian 'crusader' details months of preparation for attacks. The Washington Post, Washington (25 July)
4. Meland A, Brustad L (2011) Slik ble han terrorist på billigsalg. Dagbladet, Norway (1 Sept)
5. MacDougall I, Ritter K (2011) Norway suspect also considered other targets. Denver Post, Denver (31 July)
6. Anonymous (2010) Plane 'hijacker' had terror tip for Putin. The Moscow Times, 2 Aug. http://www.themoscowtimes.com/news/article/plane-hijacker-had-terror-tip-for-putin/411436.html. Accessed 20 Aug 2011
7. Associated Press (2007) Man admits abortion clinic bomb attempt. The Washington Post, Washington (27 July)
8. Williams C (2004) Terrorism explained. New Holland, Sydney
9. Ganor B (2002) Defining terrorism: Is one man's terrorist another man's freedom fighter? Police Pract 3(4):287–304
10. Juergensmeyer M (2000) Terror in the mind of God: the global rise of religious violence. University of California Press, Berkeley
11. Martin G (2003) Understanding terrorism: challenges, perspectives, and issues. Sage, Thousands Oaks
12. Karpin M, Friedman I (1998) Murder in the name of God: the plot to kill Yitzhak Rabin. Henry Holt and Co, New York
13. Sprinzak E (1999) Brother against brother: violence and extremism in Israeli politics from Altalena to the Rabin assassination. The Free Press, New York
14. Müller T (2006) Beestmensen: Vermomming leugens en strategie van seriemoordenaars. Mets and Schilt, Amsterdam
15. Friedrichsen G (1999) Nur irgendein Kasperl?. Der Spiegel, Hamburg, pp 184–186 (22 Feb)
16. Schwarz M (1999) Lebenslange Haft für österreichischen Bombenbauer. Berliner Zeitung, Berlin (11 March)
17. Burton F (2007) The challenge of the lone wolf. STRATFOR Global Intelligence. http://www.stratfor.com/challenge_lone_wolf. Accessed 3 August 2009
18. Oranje J (2002) Verdachte volgde Fortuyn via internet. NRC Handelsblad, The Netherlands (8 June)
19. Public Prosecution of the Netherlands (2003) Closing speech public prosecutor, 1 April. http://www.om.nl/dossier/de_zaak_fortuyn/_de_zaak_fortuyn_nieuwsberichten/21709/. Accessed 3 May 2007
20. Netherlands Broadcasting Foundation (NOS) (2004) Reconstructie van de moord. http://nos.nl/archief/2004/nieuws/index.html#@http://nos.nl/archief/2004/nieuws/dossiers/pim_fortuyn/2003/maart/2603_voorbeschouwing_proces.htm. Accessed 14 June 2007
21. Kifner J (1995) Belief to blood: the making of Rabin's killer. The New York Times, New York (19 Nov)
22. Lewis A (1995) On God's orders. The New York Times, New York (6 Nov)
23. Metropolitan Police Service (2000) Copeland case special edition. The Job, 30 June
24. Buncombe A (2000) Inspiration' came from Atlanta Olympics bomb. The Independent, 30 June
25. Metropolitan Police Service (2000) Operation marathon: Interviews with David Copeland. http://www.met.police.uk/news/stories/copeland/intervw.htm. Accessed 20 June 2007
26. BBC (2000) Transcript of BBC Panorama: the nailbomber. Recorded from transmission BBC1. BBC, London, 30 June. http://news.bbc.co.uk/hi/english/static/audio_video/programmes/panorama/transcripts/transcript_30_06_00.txt. Accessed 10 June 2007
27. Clough S (2000) Bombings 'inspired by Atlanta attack'. The Daily Telegraph, 6 June
28. Clough S (2000) Copeland took nail bomb to a park to pass the time. The Daily Telegraph, 9 June
29. Phillips P (2011) Lone wolf terrorism. Peace Econ Peace Sci Public Policy 17(1)
30. Gurr N, Cole B (2000) The new face of terrorism: threats from weapons of mass destruction. I.B. Tauris, London

31. Simon JD (2000) The alphabet bomber. In: Tucker JB (ed) Toxic terror: assessing terrorist use of chemical and biological weapons. MIT Press, Cambridge, pp 71–94
32. Laqueur W (1999) The new terrorism: fanaticism and the arms of mass destruction. Oxford University Press, Oxford
33. Spaaij R, van der Veen F (2003) NBC-terrorisme in perspectief. Het Tijdschrift voor de Politie 65(6):18–24
34. Hoffman B (2002) Rethinking terrorism and counterterrorism since 9/11. Stud Confl Terror 25(5):303–316
35. Burton F, Stewart S (2008) The 'lone wolf' disconnect. STRATFOR Global Intelligence. http://www.stratfor.com/weekly/lone_wolf_disconnect. Accessed 3 Aug 2009
36. Cruickshank P, Lister T (2011) The 'lone wolf'—The unknowable terror. CNN Security Clearance Blog, 7 Sept. http://security.blogs.cnn.com/2011/09/07/the-lone-wolf-the-unknowable-face-of-terror/. Accessed 9 Sept 2011
37. Walker C (2006) Cyber-terrorism: legal principle and law in the United Kingdom. Penn State Law Rev 110(3):625–665
38. Douglas J, Olshaker M (1999) The anatomy of motive. Scribner, New York
39. Evans PR (n.d.) Methodical terrorism: How and why. http://www.armyofgod.com/POCPaulRossEvansMethodicalTerrorism.html. Accessed 12 August 2011
40. Tuman JS (2003) Communicating terror: The rhetorical dimensions of terrorism. Sage, Thousand Oaks
41. Stewart S, Burton F (2009) Lone wolf lessons. STRATFOR Global Intelligence. http://www.stratfor.com/weekly/20090603_lone_wolf_lessons. Accessed 4 November 2010

Chapter 8
Responses

When people are targeted by a terrorist attack, among the first questions that typically follow—apart from "why?" or "why us?"—are whether the attack could have been prevented, and what should be done in response. It is therefore no surprise that the output of counterterrorism literature has dramatically accelerated, especially since 9/11. This literature shows that a wide range of counterterrorist policies and programs have been tried over the years with mixed success, and that there are substantial dissimilarities between the counterterrorism approaches of different countries depending, among other factors, on historical factors, a country's experiences with terrorism, and its political system and culture [1–6]. As will be seen, responses to lone wolf terrorism are equally context-specific, reflecting a variety of counterterrorism and police cultures and legal traditions.

At a more conceptual-analytical level, a number of studies provide a critical analysis of the options and dilemmas in responding to terrorism, with a particular focus on liberal democratic societies [7–12]. This chapter draws on insights from these studies to examine how governments and communities have responded to lone wolf terrorism, the effects of these responses, and the main lessons learned. I will specifically look at how effective responses to lone wolf terrorism might differ from effective responses to group-actor terrorism. A central tenet of the analysis is that responses to terrorism must be informed by the context within which a particular act of terrorism occurs, including the nature of the actors resorting to terrorism, the breadth and depth of their support, and even the ends they pursue [8]. Responding to terrorism here refers to any action by a (directly or indirectly) targeted interest in reply to a terrorist attack or terrorism environment [13]. As shown below, responses to lone wolf terrorism can be roughly divided into three broad categories: legalistic, repressive and conciliatory.

R. Spaaij, *Understanding Lone Wolf Terrorism*, SpringerBriefs in Criminology,
DOI: 10.1007/978-94-007-2981-0_8,

8.1 Legalistic Responses

Lone wolf terrorism is generally dealt with within existing domestic and, to a far lesser extent, international legal frameworks regarding terrorism and criminal activity. Although counterterrorism laws are typically devised or expanded following the outbreak of group-actor terrorism, there have been some instances in which (presumed) acts of lone wolf terrorism played a role in the establishment or subsequent revision of counterterrorism legislation. For example, the 1996 Anti-Terrorism and Effective Death Penalty Act in the United States was passed after Eric Rudolph's attack at Atlanta's Centennial Olympic Park during the 1996 Olympic Games, and was stimulated in part by the 1995 Oklahoma City bombing. The act allocated $1 billion to enhance federal law enforcement capacity to deter, investigate and prosecute terrorism. Among other things, the act also established a federal death penalty for terrorist murders and strengthened penalties for crimes committed against federal employees while performing their official duties.

More recently, the US government has sought to expand its powers to disrupt terrorist activities by lone individuals through the passing and subsequent extension of the Intelligence Reform and Terrorism Prevention Act in 2004, which marked a significant change to the Foreign Intelligence Surveillance Act (FISA) of 1978. The "lone wolf" provision in the new act (section 6001) allows authorities to track non-US nationals suspected of being lone wolf terrorists without confirmed ties to terrorist groups [14, 15]. The previous mandate for obtaining a foreign intelligence warrant under FISA required the government to show probable cause that the targeted individual was acting on behalf of a foreign power [16]. Under 50 U.S.C. §1801, the definition of an "agent of a foreign power" includes groups that engage in international terrorism, but does not cover unaffiliated individuals who do so. The lone wolf provision changed this definition to include all individuals who engage in international terrorism or in activities in preparation for international terrorism, regardless of whether they are connected to a terrorist group.

This 2004 amendment to FISA permits the Foreign Intelligence Surveillance Court (FISC) to issue a court order authorizing electronic surveillance and physical search orders without having to demonstrate a connection between the target of the electronic surveillance or the physical search and a foreign government or terrorist group [14, 17]. The lone wolf provision makes it significantly easier for the US government to conduct surveillance of suspected lone wolf terrorists who either act in sympathy with the aims of an international terrorist group but not on its behalf, or whose link to an international terrorist group cannot be demonstrated.

Like two other provisions in the 2004 USA Patriot Act, the lone wolf amendments constitute a temporary provision that must be periodically renewed because of concerns that they could be used to violate civil liberties. Indeed, the lone wolf provision illustrates the difficulty of finding effective solutions to minimize lone wolf terrorism which do not damage our democratic sensibilities. One could convincingly argue that emergency provisions such as these be repealed once the "crisis" has passed and that the new powers they afford to law enforcement agencies be balanced by regular checks on their impact on civil liberties. However, the recent four-year extension of the lone wolf provision (until 1 June 2015) indicates that once such a legal provision is introduced, it may be difficult to repeal, especially within the dominant discursive paradigm of the "war on terror", or what Crelinsten [12] calls "September 12 thinking". Indeed, such legislative change often becomes "the template for future actions" rather than a crisis-driven temporary emergency provision [18].

Moreover, the American Civil Liberties Union (ACLU) [19] strongly criticizes the lone wolf extension to the 2004 USA Patriot Act for not containing any privacy or civil liberties safeguards, thereby further eroding democratic civil liberties. The ACLU [20] argues that secret intelligence surveillance of foreign persons who are not affiliated with a foreign organization "is subject to abuse and threatens our long-time understandings of the limits of the government's investigatory powers within the borders of the United States". It goes on to stress that "no public records are available to document whether, or how, the government has used this power" [21, p. 14]; in others words, there is no evidence that the provision is actually an effective means to prevent lone wolf terrorism. Thus, the ACLU recommends that the lone wolf provision be allowed to expire outright. The responses highlighted above to the lone wolf provision in US federal law illustrate some of the tensions that exist between liberal democracy and counterterrorism [9, 12].

8.2 Repressive Responses

When confronted with terrorism, governments tend to turn specifically to repressive actions. Repressive responses to terrorism in liberal democracies can be categorized using two basic, increasingly blurred models: the criminal justice model and the war model [12, 22]. In the criminal justice model, terrorism is treated as crime and the police are charged with the primary responsibility for responding to terrorism. The onus of response is placed upon criminal prosecution and punishment within the rule of law [22]. In contrast, the war model regards terrorism as an act of revolutionary warfare, and places the emphasis on the military, the use of special forces, and retaliatory strikes. Whereas in the criminal justice model the rule of law is paramount, in the war model it is the rules of war that prevail [23].

While the war model has become the preferred counterterrorism approach in the post-9/11 era [12], lone wolf terrorism is typically approached from within a criminal justice model or a more hybrid model of coercion. One key reason for this is that military and paramilitary responses, such as direct military intervention, coercive covert operations and punitive or pre-emptive strikes, are highly unlikely to be effective in minimizing terrorism carried out by a single individual who may well be unknown to intelligence services, even if this individual operates transnationally (e.g. through the use of aircraft hijackings).[11] The fact is that lone wolf terrorism generally does not lend itself to military or paramilitary intervention.

In some instances, however, responses to lone wolf terrorism are characterized by a more hybrid approach that also coerces the larger communities of belief with which a lone wolf terrorist may engage. This approach recognizes that addressing wider cultures of extremism is a key aspect of countering both group-actor and solo-actor terrorism. As shown in Chap. 6, lone wolves are more often than not strongly influenced—if only tacitly or vicariously—by wider communities of support that provide ideologies which cultivate a sustained, alternate sense of morality capable of justifying terrorism. Repressive actions targeting these communities are usually undertaken by law enforcement agencies. For example, during Franz Fuchs' bombing campaign the Austrian police launched a crackdown on right-wing extremist groups in the country because they suspected that the perpetrator belonged to the far right. The neo-Nazi organization Volkstreue Außerparlamentarische Opposition (VAPO) was almost entirely eliminated. Suspected VAPO members were arrested in relation to the first series of bombings in December 1993. Along with other alleged neo-Nazis, they were eventually convicted for relatively minor offences unrelated to the bombings.

A similar yet more far-reaching response followed the assassination of Yitzhak Rabin, which fits into the expanded criminal justice model that characterizes Israel's approach to domestic right-wing terrorism [24]. The expanded criminal justice model "regards terrorism as an exceptional phenomenon and, therefore, despite the aspiration to adhere as much as possible to the rule of law, legal boundaries are extended to enable a more effective response to terrorism while partially foregoing certain liberal principles and in general abusing freedom of expression and action" [24, p. 6]. In this model, the police and secret services are accorded the primary responsibility for responding to terrorism, occasionally complemented by special anti-terrorism units. The Rabin assassination and the 1994 Hebron massacre, both of which were perpetrated by lone wolves, generated heightened awareness of the radicalization of Israel's far right. The Israeli authorities were quick to outlaw two right-wing movements (Kach and Kahane Chai) under the Prevention of Terrorism Ordinance (PTO), and movement activists were placed under the constant surveillance of the secret services. The rationale behind this response appears to have been to send a forceful message and to deny the legitimacy of these organizations. The enforcement of the PTO does not seem to have been particularly effective, however, because the cores of the movements continued under different names and exercised more caution. Pedahzur and

[11] Transnational lone wolf terrorism can be defined as involving terrorist activities carried out by individuals who are foreign based or whose activities transcend national boundaries. Franz Fuchs' bomb attacks in Austria and Germany are an example of lone wolf terrorism that transcends national boundaries, as is that by Umar Farouk Abdulmutallab, a 23-year-old Nigerian citizen who detonated an explosive device that was attached to his body aboard a flight from Amsterdam to Detroit in 2009 (see Appendix).

Ranstorp [24, p. 17] argue that these movements were easy targets for a coercive counterterrorism response due to their marginality, and because they represented, in the "outdated and entrenched" perspective of Israeli political elites and security services, the most extremist and violence-prone factions on the fringes of the Israeli far right.

Law enforcement agencies play a central role in counterterrorism operations targeting lone wolves. The role of law enforcement is multifaceted and ranges from reactive policing related to crime solving and enhanced security, to proactive policing related to terrorism detection before it happens [12]. Law enforcement responses typically include criminal investigation, specialized services (e.g. defusing and removing explosive devices), order maintenance (e.g. securing attack sites), paramilitary deployment (e.g. hostage rescue units) and security intelligence [13]. The main law enforcement approaches targeting lone wolf terrorism are discussed below.

Enhanced Security

One way in which law enforcement agencies respond to lone wolf terrorism is by enhancing security, the aim of which is to deter lone wolves from attacking likely targets. Security measures can increase the potential for failure from the terrorist's perspective, and may deter less determined and less resourceful terrorists [13]. The cases of Yigal Amir and Volkert van der Graaf illustrate this approach. The murder of Yitzhak Rabin sparked fierce debate on Rabin's security and the operations of the Israeli security services [25, 26]. The threat of political assassination by a Jewish extremist was understood months before Rabin was killed. A few weeks before the assassination, Rabin narrowly escaped assault as a man who rushed toward him in a crowd was pushed away and tackled by security agents [27]. As noted in Chap. 7, Amir himself had set out to kill Rabin three times before. One report about a possible assassination of Rabin came from two friends of Amir—Hila Frank and Shlomi Halevy. Frank had repeatedly heard Amir speak of the obligation to kill the Prime Minister, but she did not normally take him seriously. On one occasion, however, Amir told Frank of his readiness to kill the Prime Minister and of a confession he had made in the synagogue. After Frank deliberated the issue with Shlomi Halevy, who served in Israel's military intelligence, the two decided to inform the authorities. Since they were friends of Amir and unsure of the seriousness of his statements, they reported the matter without identifying Amir by name. The information was passed on to Israeli security, which filed it without further investigation. The security service later explained that it had received hundreds of similar warning signals and was unable to pursue all of them. As it turned out, Rabin was not well protected during the peace rally in Tel Aviv. The VIP parking lot was not sealed off from the crowd, and although Rabin had several bodyguards, it appears that they were not alert [26]. In the aftermath of the Rabin assassination, the security services stepped up security around Acting Prime Minister Shimon Peres, who received several extra bodyguards.

The assassination of Pim Fortuyn by Volkert van der Graaf raised similar debate and resulted in an official inquiry into the Dutch government's responsibility and capacity to protect its politicians. The commission charged with the inquiry concluded that the Dutch intelligence service and national police force had functioned poorly in relation to Fortuyn's protection and that the Dutch government should have provided Fortuyn with adequate personal security [28]. The commission found that although individuals are principally responsible for their own safety, when they are unable to protect themselves the government should provide adequate protection. Nevertheless, it was stressed that complete safety cannot be guaranteed even where such protection is in place. The commission recommended that the existing *Stelsel Bewaken en Beveiligen* (Protection and Security System) be significantly revised, for example with regard to the criteria for and coordination of protection and security [28]. To implement and coordinate these changes, in 2003 a national coordinator was appointed within the Justice Department. In 2005 the Justice and Home Affairs Ministers evaluated the *Stelsel Bewaken en Beveiligen* and expanded the list of individuals, objects and organizations for which the Dutch government has a special responsibility in terms of protection and security. In the aftermath of the Fortuyn assassination, a number of politicians were granted protection.

Although the security measures put in place in the aftermath of the Rabin and Fortuyn assassinations may have deterred some like-minded individuals from targeting high-profile politicians, the effectiveness of increased security measures aimed at hardening terrorism targets should not be overstated. Improved security in some areas may have the unintended side effect of encouraging lone wolf terrorists to attack other, "softer" targets, or to devise tactics to circumvent these precautions [29]. Moreover, the question is how far this quest for enhanced security should go. As Sederberg [7, p. 145] notes, "the fear of terrorism can induce a mania for security that undermines the very character of the political system presumably being defended". Thus, the vision of total security is not only unrealizable, but erodes the very nature of the type of society we seek to defend [30].

Intelligence

A major strand in proactive policing responses to lone wolf terrorism is the collection and analysis of intelligence in order to prevent terrorism. Clearly, an optimal outcome of counterterrorist intelligence is the ability to anticipate the behaviour of terrorists and to predict and disrupt planned terrorist attacks. However, although intelligence is considered useful for generalized prediction, it is less useful for predicting the precise location and timing of terrorist attacks [13]. Moreover, lone wolf terrorism can be even more difficult to detect and prevent than group-actor terrorism. Preventing a lone wolf terrorist attack through the use of intelligence is complicated by five key factors:

- Lone wolf terrorists operate alone and tend to be secretive about their operations;
- There may be few clear warning signs before lone wolf terrorists strike because they are likely to be relatively socially isolated and may avoid contact with others;
- They display a variety of backgrounds with a wide spectrum of ideologies and motivations, which makes it difficult to predict from which environment they stem;
- It is extremely difficult to differentiate between those extremists who intend to commit attacks and those who simply express radical beliefs;
- Many lone wolves carry out only one attack, rather than a more prolonged terrorist campaign characteristic of most group-actor terrorism.

Although in retrospect it is often possible to identify early warning signs that could have been picked up by law enforcement agencies prior to a lone wolf terrorist attack, it is much harder to gather and accurately assess such intelligence beforehand due in part to these five factors. It is in this context that Europol [31, p. 15] states that the activities of lone wolves "can be unpredictable and difficult to prevent". Shone [32] goes even further by asserting the "infinite unpredictability of their threat". Indeed, preventing a lone wolf terrorist attack would often require a sophisticated intelligence system covering all actual or potential extremist milieus and all vulnerable people and objects, which would be costly and further infringe on civil liberties, and still be no guarantee for success.

Notwithstanding these limitations, the collection and analysis of intelligence is clearly a central aspect of responses aimed at minimizing lone wolf terrorism. In an environment where potential threats are hard to identify, intelligence-led operations must focus on the "how" rather than the "who", that is, on individuals' *behaviour* and knowing how attacks are formulated [32–34]. As Thomas Müller, the criminal psychologist who investigated Franz Fuchs' bombing campaign, states: "We do not search for offenders, we look for offender behaviours" [35]. Thus, in the aftermath of the 22 July 2011 attacks in Norway, the question emerged as to what the authorities could have done to identify or prevent the accused perpetrator's purchases of bomb-making ingredients and specialist weaponry as well as other suspect behaviour.

Lone wolf terrorist attacks are usually preceded by a careful and protracted preparatory phase (see Chap. 7). Lone wolves are thus vulnerable to detection at several different stages of their attack cycle, notably in the planning stage when weapons are acquired and in the surveillance of their targets [36]. This period can provide security intelligence with some indicators in relation to the (attempted) purchase of firearms or (large quantities of) ingredients for improvised explosive devices, or suspicious entries on social networking, chat or hate websites [37]. To this end, law enforcement agencies use several strategies to gather intelligence on potential terrorist plots by lone individuals including, among other things, undercover operations, the analysis of CCTV footage, and the monitoring of Internet and library activity [38, 39]. Being in contact with communities is often key for police and intelligence agencies in gathering early warnings of threats. Intelligence on prospective lone wolf terrorist activities relies heavily on information provided by the public (e.g. witnesses, family members, friends or work colleagues) and businesses. There have been a number of occasions where law enforcement agencies were only alerted to an alleged lone wolf terrorist plot after reports from store owners or online companies on suspicious purchases (e.g. chemical supplies or guns) [38]. However, as the Amir case discussed earlier in this chapter clearly shows, whether this information will contribute to the detection of a lone wolf terrorist depends not only on the quality of the information provided, but also on its subsequent analysis and follow-up.

The cases of David Copeland and Franz Fuchs illustrate how intelligence-led responses to lone wolf terrorism can be effective. The investigation by the Anti-Terrorist Branch of the Metropolitan Police, codenamed "Operation Marathon", led to the arrest of David Copeland in a remarkably short period of time, which probably prevented further attacks. Copeland confessed that he had Peckham, Southall and Tottenham, all multicultural areas, on his list of future targets [40]. The criminal investigation commenced immediately after the first bombing in Brixton with the scanning of 26,000 hours of CCTV footage covering the Brixton area. Police officers were able to recover the black sports bag in which the bomb had been planted, and began to search the footage for people carrying bags of that type. This eventually led to identification of a man who had been carrying the exact sports bag. On 29 April 1999 the police released CCTV images of Copeland to the media, which led to hundreds of calls from members of the public with information relating to potential suspects. Over 1,600 statements were taken [41]. A taxi driver rang the Anti-Terrorist Hotline to report that he had picked up a man fitting the description from Waterloo station the previous Saturday. CCTV footage from cameras at Waterloo station indicated that the suspect had travelled by train from the direction of Hampshire. Eighty minutes before the third bomb went off in Soho, a man alerted police that one of his work colleagues closely resembled the suspect. That same night the police planned the raid on Copeland's home where he was subsequently arrested [42].

The criminal investigation of Franz Fuchs' bombing campaign featured the close involvement of criminal psychologists and behavioural scientists, with psychologist Thomas Müller playing a significant role in the search for the bomber. Müller and the Austrian authorities developed a five-phase program to identify Fuchs by means of a "psychological duel" [43, 44]. The first phase consisted of attempts to acknowledge the skills of the bomber in public statements by police, stressing his detailed knowledge of electronics, physics and chemistry. The next phase was to install a "bad conscious" into the perpetrator. In one of Fuchs's letters, Müller found indications that the bomber liked small children. Consequently, Müller visited a neo-Nazi who was suspected of the bombings but imprisoned for other offences, and recorded the man's complaints about the fact that he had not been permitted to see his newborn daughter while in prison. Müller forwarded the recording to the media, hoping to make Fuchs feel responsible for the man not being able to see his child. During the third phase, the authorities provided two journalists with inside information and photographs of the crime scenes. The journalists wrote a book that included Müller's profile of the bomber [45]. According to this profile, the perpetrator was an Austrian male aged in his 50s who had probably completed secondary education and lived in a family house. The profile further stated that the perpetrator possessed specialized tools and a hobby workplace, was a Catholic, and had knowledge of hierarchies and religious titles. He also had knowledge of chemistry and an interest in history, liked order and tidiness, and was extremely precise. Police hoped that the bomber would read the book and that this would increase his stress levels and force him to make an error [35]. However, the book was never found among his possessions [46].

During the fourth phase of the investigation, the Austrian government announced that it would introduce the legal arrangements for the strategy of *Rasterfahndung* ("dragnet") in order to identify the bomber, giving police more powers to collect intelligence. *Rasterfahndung* refers to a large-scale data comparison operation that systematically searches and links different databases on the basis of a terrorist or criminal profile, and has been a central yet controversial element of German counterterrorism policy since the 1970s [47, 48]. The *Rasterfahndung* policy was put into practice in Austria on 1 October 1997. In the final phase of the program, the government publicly stated that ten Austrian citizens had emerged from the investigation as potential perpetrators, and that these persons were under close and continuous surveillance [44].

The Austrian authorities believed that the five-phase program and criminal investigation significantly increased Franz Fuchs' stress levels [35]. The now 48-year-old Fuchs had been taking notes and photographs of people and cars that passed his house. On the same night the *Rasterfahndung* policy was introduced, two women coincidentally drove past Fuchs's house twice. Believing the women to be undercover police officers, Fuchs jumped in his car and began to follow them. One of the women called the police to report the stalking. When police officers stopped him near Leibnitz, Fuchs tried to commit suicide using an improvised explosive device, as he was convinced that they were about to arrest him in relation to the bombings. His suicide attempt failed, but he lost both hands and injured a nearby police officer [49]. According to Müller [43], the program designed to identify the bomber had clearly increased the pressure on Fuchs. However, it was a mere coincidence and luck that the two women drove past Fuchs's home twice that night [50].

Two important lessons can be learned from these cases. The first lesson is that non-military pressure in terms of the public release of a profile, image or composite sketch of the suspect can be effective in disrupting lone wolf terrorism and increasing the chance of detection. The investigation into Theodore Kaczynski's bombing campaign further validates this point. In 1987 the FBI released a sketch of the Unabomber suspect based on a witness description. The bombings stopped immediately and Kaczynski remained inactive for six years while the investigation continued. On the other hand, public release of such information may also have unintended consequences. For example, David Copeland responded by bringing forward his third bombing attack by a day, killing three people before the police could arrest him. The second lesson to be learned here is that, as Thomson [51, p. 30] notes, "luck plays a large part in counterterrorism efforts". At least in the short term, luck can well be as important as good intelligence in detecting or disrupting lone wolf terrorism. However, as the cases of Franz Fuchs and David Copeland demonstrate, more often than not luck appears to be "the byproduct of solid planning and adept policy implementation" [51, p. 30].

The inherent difficulties in the collection and analysis of intelligence mean that its importance as an effective response to lone wolf terrorism should not be overstated. Despite some significant successes in detecting or disrupting lone wolf terrorism, there have been a number of cases in which intelligence operations failed to provide a tactical warning of an attempted lone wolf terrorist attack or to identify the perpetrator of a series of attacks. Take, for example, the investigation into Theodore Kaczynski's 18-year bombing campaign. The FBI launched one of its longest and most expensive domestic investigations to identify and capture Kaczynski. Over the years a number of offender profiles were developed in order to identify the bomber. The breakthrough in the investigation came only after Kaczynski, who was particularly obsessed with publicity and concerned that his actions would be misunderstood [52], sent his 35,000-word manifesto to *The New York Times*. Kaczynski promised that he would renounce terrorism if his manifesto were published. After long and careful deliberation, the *Washington Post* and *The New York Times* decided to co-publish the manifesto in September 1995, based on the Justice Department's recommendation to publish the material out of a concern for public safety [53]. FBI agents also sent copies of the manifesto to professors in the Chicago area to see if any of them remembered a former student who made similar arguments or matched the profile. An FBI taskforce concluded that the bomber was probably exposed to the history of science, or some related discipline, in the late 1970s in the Chicago area, as this was the area where the Unabomber began his bombing campaign [53].

David Kaczynski read the Unabomber's manifesto in the newspapers and recognized the similarities between the published manifesto and the writings of his older brother Theodore. After contacting the family attorney and handwriting experts, David Kaczynski eventually contacted the FBI. By February 1996, investigators began staking out Theodore Kaczynski's cabin near Lincoln, Montana, where he had been living in self-imposed exile for more than 25 years. He was arrested by FBI agents disguised as local mountain men on 3 April 1996. In retrospect, had Kaczynski not been as obsessed with publicity as he was, he might never have been unmasked and arrested [54].

Internet Surveillance

For the above reasons, then, the function of intelligence in responses to lone wolf terrorism is central but inevitably modest: it is a prerequisite for an effective policy or strategy, but it can never be a substitute for these elements [55]. Furthermore, one could ask how far an intelligence-led response to lone wolf terrorism should go, given both its cost and limitations, and its infringement on civil liberties. The usual response to intelligence failure is to call for more and better intelligence, but such calls tend to ignore the inherent complexities, shortcomings and dilemmas of the collection and analysis of intelligence for counterterrorist purposes [12]. The monitoring of radical websites and their users, known as "cybersurveillance" or "cyber intelligence", is a case in point. Many governments have sought ways to limit or minimize terrorists' use of the Internet. In theory this strategy seems reasonable given that, as discussed in Chap. 6, the Internet makes it easier for any alienated loner to make contact with radical material or like-minded individuals. However, its effectiveness is not only constrained by the fact that it is extremely difficult to differentiate between those extremists who intend to commit attacks and those who simply express radical beliefs, but raises the important question of how monitoring of the Internet can be done without interfering with civil liberties such as freedom of speech.

The close monitoring of Internet fora and the removal of specific websites from the Internet appear to be relatively futile attempts to restrict terrorists' access and exposure, even though the monitoring of online extremist communities and hate websites can help to develop an understanding of the ideological environments from within which a lone wolf terrorist may emerge. Weimann [56] proposes a strategy that seeks to strike a balance between security and liberty, accepting both some vulnerabilities of the Internet to terrorism and some constraints on civil liberties. Weimann [56, pp. 224–242] recommends modifying legislation (including the USA Patriot Act) to transform Internet surveillance laws into a "public pact" between society, government and security agencies, encouraging self-policing on the Internet, and promoting peaceful uses of the Internet, among other approaches. As part of this strategy, the Internet's potential for virtual diplomacy and nonviolent management of conflicts ought to be highlighted and embraced. Weimann's proposed strategy underlines the significance of conciliatory responses to terrorism, which will be explored later in this chapter.

Emergency Preparedness and Resilience

Lone wolf terrorism will continue to occur and it will not always be possible to anticipate and prevent such attacks. For this reason, it is important to invest in emergency preparedness and resilience to minimize the impact of an attack and to enable society to bounce back and recover. In the aftermath of the 22 July 2011 attacks in Norway, the Norwegian police came under scrutiny for the slow pace of their response to the incidents and the seemingly poor protection of the targeted government buildings [57–60]. It took the special operations team nearly 90 minutes to reach the scene of the mass shooting. Police were already grappling with the damage inflicted by the bomb attack in central Oslo when word of the shootings on the island of Utøya came. The special operations team then had to drive to the scene of the attack rather than take a helicopter because all police helicopter pilots were on summer holidays. The first boat they tried to take to the island broke down, forcing the ten commandos involved in the operation to take two civilian boats instead. When they reached the gunman, the accused perpetrator Breivik immediately dropped his guns and surrendered [60]. Critics argue that the delayed response likely cost dozens of lives [57]. Whilst at the time of writing there are still many unanswered questions (which will be investigated by the official July 22 Commission), the criticism of the Norwegian police highlights the need for a quick law enforcement and emergency response to (multiple) terrorist incidents that is well prepared, well equipped in terms of human resources and technical capabilities, and regularly exercised.

In a context where anticipation and predictability are low, resilience is of great import. Lone wolf terrorism is one such context. Anticipation refers to efforts made to predict and prevent potential dangers before damage is done. In contrast, resilience is "the capacity to cope with unanticipated dangers after they have become manifest, learning to bounce back" [61, p. 77]. Put differently, while anticipation attempts to avoid possible hazards, resilience is concerned with those dangers that have been realized. The importance of resilience is widely recognized in the counterterrorism and disaster management literature. For example, Coaffee [62] asserts that the search for appropriate counterterrorism and security solutions has led to the adoption of a new vocabulary centred on resilience, which is at once proactive and reactive, with an in-built adaptability to the fluid nature of the new terrorism threats. In recent years, the concept of resilience has been professionalized and turned into a tool for risk and disaster management. In so doing, the process of developing resilience is often uprooted from its social context and community setting and comes to rely first and foremost on professional intervention and training [63]. One of the main problems with this conceptualization of resilience, however, as Furedi [63, p. 183] rightly notes, is that it uses resilience "in a way that presupposes the primacy of vulnerability". Furedi [63, p. 183] argues that a technocratic orientation towards resilience typically seeks to institutionalize a top-down professional approach that leaves little room for local initiative, and is therefore "unlikely to engage the creative and problem-solving capacities of communities" who are faced with a violent threat to their life. This issue is further explored below in the discussion of conciliatory responses to lone wolf terrorism.

8.3 Conciliatory Responses

The dominant response to lone wolf terrorism consists of repressive actions such as criminal investigation, increased security and surveillance. As noted earlier, the advantages and disadvantages of the application of repressive measures need to be considered very carefully, and it must be recognized that the law enforcement solution by itself is inevitably incomplete [9]. The inclination to overvalue the effectiveness of repressive responses often goes hand in hand with a tendency to dismiss the efficacy of democratic responses [8]. It would be foolish, however, to dismiss conciliatory responses out of hand. Instead, we must determine how and when they might work, and also how they might be used in conjunction with repressive responses.

The short-term conciliatory response to lone wolf terrorism is to accede to the immediate demands of the perpetrator in order to end a particular terrorist incident or campaign. A policy of short-term concessions presumes that the perpetrators make reasonably concrete demands. Crucially, the costs and risks of concessions must be balanced against potential benefits [7]. For example, it may be sensible to exchange a small concession for the safe release of hostages and the peaceful surrender of the perpetrator. The aircraft hijacking by Hussein Shey Kholya in 1983 is a case in point (see Chap. 7 and Appendix). Kholya released all 21 passengers and crew members after striking a deal with Mexican officials for a plane ticket to Cuba in exchange for the release of the hostages. All hostages were unharmed.

In many cases, however, the consequences of concessions are difficult to foresee. Earlier in this chapter, I argued that had Theodore Kaczynski's manifesto not been published, he might never have been arrested. At the time, however, newspaper editors and media analysts were divided on whether *The New York Times* and *Washington Post* should print the Unabomber's manifesto. Some commentators believed that publishing a 35,000-word manifesto was a small price to pay for the possibility that the perpetrator would halt his attacks on people as he had promised. Others warned that the media had no way of knowing whether the perpetrator would keep his word and that accepting his terms could encourage violent groups to make similar demands [53].

The question of whether lone wolf terrorists should be granted the oxygen of publicity on which they often thrive is complex and multifaceted. Indeed, many lone wolf terrorists long for their voices to be heard: they want people to know about their plight and believe that they are the vanguard to the cause. As we have seen in previous chapters, it is relatively common for lone wolf terrorists to communicate with their audiences not just through violence, but through statements, letters, manifestos or videos sent to news media or posted on the Internet. Communicating the threat of terrorism to relevant target audiences while at the same time refraining from handing lone wolves the public voice they strive for, is a major challenge for counterterrorism actors [64]. One main risk is that concessions of this type facilitate a contamination or inspiration effect; that is, they can inspire copycat behaviour where lone wolf terrorists become role models for other alienated individuals and invite bandwagon attacks (e.g. [65]). In previous chapters we have seen some examples of copycat-type behaviours, for example by David Copeland who stated that he was inspired by Eric Rudolph [66, 67]. Furthermore, in his manifesto the accused lone wolf terrorist Anders Breivik writes that he sought to inspire others to carry out similar attacks elsewhere. This issue touches upon a fundamental challenge for counterterrorism: how to effectively respond to lone wolf terrorism without instilling fear in society or further alienating those susceptible to violent radicalization. It is to this challenge that I will now turn.

Long-term strategies of (re)conciliation can prove quite capable of mitigating some of the underlying grievances and isolating extreme elements from their more moderate supporters. One way in which this can be done is through social reforms, especially where terrorists' objectives are more limited, reasonably concrete and widely supported [7]. Indeed, not all actors using terrorism have unlimited political agendas, and rhetoric of total destruction of their antagonists often defies reality [8]. Reforms can include, *inter alia*, the improvement of socioeconomic conditions, increased political rights, government recognition of ethno-nationalist or religious sentiment, or public recognition of the validity of grievances [13]. Conciliatory responses of this nature also apply to those who have not yet fully radicalized towards terrorist violence. For example, Demant et al. [68, p. 186] recommend that the wishes of radical individuals "be seriously listened to and examined to see whether these do indeed contain legitimate social criticism which could actually improve society". In this context, Sederberg [8, p. 279] argues that repressive actions may be most plausible against isolated fringe groups, while "conciliatory strategies increase in relevance as the base of support for the adversary expands". In other words, responses to terrorism must be informed by the context within which it occurs, including the nature of the terrorist actors, the breadth and depth of their support, and even the ends they pursue.

At first sight, one could conclude from this that lone wolf terrorism is most effectively countered through punitive actions because lone wolf terrorists lack a broad base of support. However, as has been reiterated throughout this treatise, lone wolf terrorism does not take place in a social vacuum. As shown in Chap. 6, the vast majority of lone wolves exhibit a degree of identification with extremist movements and communities of support. Because of this, counter-narratives are an important element of a comprehensive response strategy aimed at counter-radicalization. To this end, Shone [32] proposes that governments work collaboratively with communities to ensure that alienation is reduced and non-radical (democratic) ideologies are propagated, thus delegitimizing extremists. This approach resonates with recent research [68] which shows that ideology and a search for meaning are key (but not the only) factors in both violent radicalization *and* de-radicalization. This research stresses the need for, *inter alia*, stimulating the democratic approach and the openness and inclusiveness of society, limiting isolation, and opening democratic paths and social opportunities.

Conciliatory responses of this kind are of course not without limitations. Considering the variety of individual trajectories and motives that underlie the violent radicalization of lone wolf terrorists, it is highly unlikely that one size will fit all when it comes to conciliatory and preventive measures aimed at counter-radicalization. Furthermore, whilst ideology is often an important factor in violent radicalization, lone wolf terrorists tend to create *personalized* ideologies that combine broader political, religious or social aims with personal frustrations and aversion. What this means is that their demands may not have a broad base of support or be under-defined, and it is therefore extremely difficult to implement social reforms to meet these demands. Moreover, even where this would be theoretically possible, the more ambitious demands of lone wolf terrorists cannot usually be met within a democratic framework guided by the rule of law. Consider for example accused perpetrator Anders Breivik's declaration of war against Muslims and progressive governments or David Copeland's "racial war" against Black and minority ethnic populations, both of which call for the annihilation of the enemy. In a similar vein, the demands of lone wolf jihadi terrorists who call for a total war on "the West", "Crusaders" or "Zionists" cannot be met by democratic means.

In this context, it is useful to reconsider the concept of inversion discussed at length in Chap. 6. Wieviorka [69] argues that the pathway into terrorism involves, among other things, the inversion of the principle of totality, which ceases to be a reference to a concrete cause and manifests itself in a life-or-death combat that calls for the destruction of the existing order. In the process, the terrorist actor exits the political arena with no thought of ever returning. This suggests that democratic counter-narratives and other forms of long-term conciliatory response are far more likely to affect those who have not yet fully radicalized towards terrorism than those who have reached the point of no return, especially when the latter are lone individuals with poorly defined agendas.

Despite these important qualifications, the conciliatory responses outlined above must not be undervalued. A key strength of conciliatory strategies is their emphasis on the efficacy of democratic responses, a capacity that is often dismissed by those who advocate repressive coercion [8]. Whilst not denying the need for lessened vulnerability (security) and interdiction of planned attacks (intelligence), the key point here is that any response to terrorism must be based on democratic principles and respect for human rights [9]. Sederberg [7] rightly notes that rather than bemoaning how the key virtues of a constitutional democracy—that is, relative openness, commitment to the rule of law, the representativeness of its institutions, and its capacity for responsive reform—handcuff the authorities in their response to terrorism, we should look to ways of strengthening them because they stand as more certain barriers against terrorism. Indeed, as Brysk [70] argues, democracy is actually the best basis for a long-term response.

The Norwegian authorities' initial responses to the 22 July 2011 attacks underline this argument. Notwithstanding the aforementioned scrutiny of the Norwegian police, overall the criticism of both the government and the country's police and security forces has been muted, and the dominant response has been to express wholehearted support for the democratic values of Norwegian society [30]. Although new security measures will most likely be implemented, the Norwegian authorities are well aware of the costs of such measures, which are deemed to fit uneasily within Norway's existing culture of openness and trust. Prime Minister Jens Stoltenberg has been hailed for responding to the espoused ideology of the accused perpetrator of the 22 July attacks by stating that "the Norwegian response to violence is more democracy, more openness and greater political participation" [18]. Stoltenberg went on to assert: "It's absolutely possible to have an open, democratic, inclusive society, and at the same time have security measures and not be naïve. … I hope and also believe that the Norway we will see after [22 July] will be more open, a more tolerant society than what we had before" [57]. In a similar vein, the director of Norway's national security agency PST, Janne Kristiansen, stated that "the trick is to make it easier to catch this kind of person without taking away the openness and liberties more than necessary" [71]. Furthermore, when asked whether Oslo needs greater security to prevent future terrorist attacks, Mayor Fabian Stang replied: "I don't think security can solve problems. We need to teach greater respect" [18].

What these responses suggest is that while the Norwegian authorities intend to investigate what exactly happened in the attacks and correct any needed gaps in security and emergency preparedness, their primary response is "defined by a belief that there are other values besides security that matter a great deal and that pursuing security above all other values, in a quest for absolute safety, is both self-destructive and futile" [18]. Kristian Berg Harpviken [30], the director of the Peace Research Institute Oslo, eloquently expresses this belief:

> The very best protection against future acts of terrorism in Norway will involve maintaining the openness and trust that characterizes Norwegian society and government, leaving room for the expression of political views of many different kinds. We cannot remove dangers through regulations and control. Such measures will not save us from the dangers of violent extremism and terrorism. Through it may be very demanding, we have to learn to live with risk. This is part of being human, part of being a society.

Key to this response, then, is a refusal to be terrorized. According to Furedi [63], this type of response is in fact the most effective way of countering and minimizing the threat of terrorism. Furedi [63] argues that "the message that is all too often communicated by official sources, that terrorism can strike any place and any time, is not only fundamentally wrong, it also plays in the hands of those threatening to inflict violence." A defensive and fearful reaction to the threat of terrorism represents "an open invitation to be terrorized" [63, p. 174]. The point here is that terrorist attacks succeed in so far as the target society responds in the way the perpetrators of these acts intended. The more accurate response, Furedi asserts, is to accept that while acts of terrorism cannot always be prevented and can be shocking, painful and costly, they are a "normal" and manageable risk among other risks. Open societies are vulnerable to discrete acts of terrorism, but terrorism "cannot seriously threaten the integrity of society nor undermine the way of life of a nation" [63, p. 171].

Refusing to be terrorized is an important response to lone wolf terrorism. Despite the increase in the incidence of lone wolf terrorism over time, acts of lone wolf terrorism remain rather rare, at an average rate of 4.7 attacks per year across all 15 countries in the research sample combined (see Chap. 4). Moreover, lone wolf terrorism is not generally a very destructive phenomenon, indicative of which is the low lethality rate of lone wolf terrorist attacks, which averages around 0.62 fatalities per incident. In addition, there is no evidence that the overall lethality of lone wolf terrorism is on the increase. Clearly, in certain conditions the impact of lone wolf terrorism can be relatively large, for instance when lone wolf terrorists assassinate political leaders, a deed that is often regarded by the public as an attack not only on the victim, but on the socio-political structure the victim represents [72]. Overall, however, the vast majority of people have had no direct experience of lone wolf terrorism, and the chances of you being hurt by a lone wolf terrorist attack are minimal.

Although the 22 July 2011 attacks in Norway are an important reminder that acts of lone wolf terrorism clearly do have shocking, painful and costly ramifications, particularly for the families and friends of the victims, these attacks are exceptional in terms of their destructiveness. We need to recognize that the accused perpetrator of the Norwegian attacks stands in contrast to most lone wolf terrorists in terms of their capability to inflict serious damage on a comparatively large scale. While lone wolf terrorism has been propagated and executed for many years now, there have been relatively few successful attacks [33], and even fewer attacks cause significant destruction and loss of life.

References

1. Schmid AP, Crelinsten RD (eds) (1993) Western responses to terrorism. Frank Cass, London
2. Alexander Y (ed) (2002) Combating terrorism: Strategies of ten countries. University of Michigan Press, Ann Arbor
3. van Leeuwen M (ed) (2003) Confronting terrorism: European experiences threat perceptions and policies. Kluwer, The Hague
4. von Hippel K (ed) (2005) Europe confronts terrorism. Palgrave, London
5. TTSRL (2008) Radicalisation, recruitment and the EU counter-radicalisation strategy. European Commission Sixth Framework program Transnational Terrorism, Security and the Rule of Law, Brussels
6. TTSRL (2008) Mapping counterterrorism. European Commission Sixth Framework program Transnational Terrorism, Security and the Rule of Law, Brussels
7. Sederberg PC (1989) Terrorist myths: illusion, rhetoric, and reality. Prentice-Hall, Englewood Cliffs
8. Sederberg PC (2003) Global terrorism: problems of challenge and response. In: Kegley CW Jr (ed) The new global terrorism: characteristics, causes, controls. Prentice Hall, Upper Saddle River, pp 267–284
9. Wilkinson P (2006) Terrorism versus democracy: the liberal state response, 2nd edn. Routledge, London
10. Brysk A, Shafir G (eds) (2007) National insecurity and human rights: Democracies debate counterterrorism. University of California Press, Berkeley
11. Bianchi A, Keller A (eds) (2008) Counterterrorism: democracy's challenge. Hart Publishing, Portland
12. Crelinsten RD (2009) Counterterrorism. Polity, Cambridge
13. Martin G (2003) Understanding terrorism: challenges, perspectives, and issues. Sage, Thousands Oaks
14. Bazan EB (2004) Intelligence reform and terrorism prevention act of 2004: 'lone wolf'amendment to the foreign intelligence surveillance act. CRS report for Congress. Congressional Research Service, Washington
15. Al Jazeera (2011) Obama signs patriot act extension. Al Jazeera, 27 May. http://english.aljazeera.net/news/americas/2011/05/201152715850301322.html. Accessed 9 July 2011

16. Scahill T (2006) The domestic security enhancement act of 2003: a glimpse into a post-patriot act approach to combating domestic terrorism. CR: New Centennial Rev 6(1):69–94
17. Bellia PL (2005) The 'lone wolf' amendment and the future of foreign intelligence surveillance law. Villanova Law Rev 50:425–455
18. Greenwald G (2011) An un-American response to the Oslo attack. Salon.com, 28 July. http://www.salon.com/news/opinion/glenn_greenwald/2011/07/28/norway. Accessed 29 July 2011
19. American Civil Liberties Union (2011) House passes extension of overbroad patriot act provisions. http://www.aclu.org/national-security/house-passes-extension-overbroad-patriot-act-provisions. Accessed 20 Aug 2011
20. American Civil Liberties Union (2011) Patriot Act: Eight years later. http://www.reformthepatriotact.org/. Accessed 20 August 2011
21. American Civil Liberties Union (2009) Reclaiming patriotism: a call to reconsider the patriot act. ACLU, New York
22. Crelinsten RD, Schmid AP (1993) Western responses to terrorism: a twenty-five year balance sheet. In: Schmid AP, Crelinsten RD (eds) Western responses to terrorism. Frank Cass, London, pp 307–340
23. Crelinsten RD (1998) The discourse and practice of counter-terrorism in liberal democracies. Aust J Politics Hist 44(1):389–413
24. Pedahzur A, Ranstorp M (2001) A tertiary model for countering terrorism in liberal democracies: the case of Israel. Terrorism Political Violence 13(2):1–26
25. Karpin M, Friedman I (1998) Murder in the name of God: the plot to kill Yitzhak Rabin. Henry Holt and Co, New York
26. Sprinzak E (1999) Brother against brother: violence and extremism in Israeli politics from Altalena to the Rabin assassination. The Free Press, New York
27. Rodgers W (1995) Anti-Rabin sentiment had turned ugly: confessed assassin had been seen before. CNN World News, 5 November. http://www.cnn.com/WORLD/9511/rabin/why_now/index.html. Accessed 9 June 2007
28. Commissie Van den Haak (2002) De veiligheid en beveiliging van Pim Fortuyn: Feiten en verantwoordelijkheden. SDU Uitgevers, The Hague
29. Brandt P, Sandler T (2010) What do transnational terrorists target? Has it changed? Are we safer? J Conflict Resolut 54(2):214–236
30. Harpviken KB (2011) Norway after the terror. Plato's Cave Blog, 1 August. http://platoscaveblog.wordpress.com/2011/08/01/norway-after-the-terror/. Accessed 5 Aug 2011
31. Europol (2011) TE-SAT 2011: EU terrorism situation and trend report. Europol, The Hague
32. Shone A (2010) Countering lone wolf terrorism: sustaining the CONTEST vision. http://www.henryjacksonsociety.org/stories.asp?id=1582. Accessed 12 Aug 2011
33. Stewart S (2011) Norway: lessons from a successful lone wolf attacker. STRATFOR Global Intelligence. http://www.stratfor.com/weekly/20110727-norway-lessons-successful-lone-wolf-attacker. Accessed 30 July 2011
34. Stewart S (2011) Al Qaeda's new video: a message of defeat. STRATFOR Global Intelligence. http://www.stratfor.com/weekly/20110608-AlQaedas-new-video-message-defeat. Accessed 30 July 2011
35. Brock P (1999) The profiling method(s): interview mit Thomas Müller. Berliner Zeitung, 29 December
36. Stewart S, Burton F (2008) Lone wolf lessons. STRATFOR Global Intelligence. http://www.stratfor.com/weekly/20090603_lone_wolf_lessons. Accessed 4 Nov 2010
37. Williams C (2011) Deadly, cruel lesson from Norway. The Australian, 26 July 11
38. Temple-Raston D (2010) Lone-wolf plots alter anti-terrorism strategy in US. National Public Radio, 30 December. http://www.npr.org/2010/12/30/132447190/lone-wolf-plotsalter-u-s-anti-terrorism-strategy. Accessed 6 Aug 2011
39. Cruickshank P, Lister T (2011) The 'lone wolf'—the unknowable terror. CNN Security Clearance Blog, 7 September. http://security.blogs.cnn.com/2011/09/07/the-lone-wolf-the-unknowable-face-of-terror/. Accessed 9 Sept 2011

40. Clough S (2000) Copeland took nail bomb to a park to pass the time. The Daily Telegraph, 9 June
41. Metropolitan Police Service (2000) Copeland case special edition. The Job, 30 June
42. Hopkins N, Hall S (2000) David copeland: a quiet introvert, obsessed with Hitler and bombs. The Guardian, 30 June. http://www.guardian.co.uk/uk/2000/jun/30/uksecurity.sarahhall
43. Müller T (2006) Beestmensen: vermomming leugens en strategie van seriemoordenaars. Mets & Schilt, Amsterdam
44. von Goos H (2005) Der Großwildjäger. Der Spiegel, 3 January
45. Grassl-Kosa M, Steiner H (1996) Der Briefbomber ist unter uns. GKS, Wien
46. Pühringer M (2003) Briefbomben: universalgenie franz fuchs? http://www.wienweb.at/content.aspx?id=59329&channel=2&cat=32. Accessed 17 June 2007
47. TTSRL (2007) The evolving threat of terrorism in policymaking and media discourse. European Commission Sixth Framework program Rransnational Terrorism, Security and the Rule of Law, Brussels
48. Heinz W (2007) Germany: State responses to terrorist challenges and human rights. In: Brysk A, Shafir G (eds) National insecurity and human rights: democracies debate counterterrorism. University of California Press, Berkeley, pp 157–176
49. Friedrichsen G (1999) Nur irgendein Kasperl? Der Spiegel. 22 February, pp 184–186
50. Mappes-Niediek N (1997) Zufall führte zum österreichischen 'Bombenhirn'. Berliner Zeitung, 4 October
51. Thomson JA (2007) Beating the odds: In the war on terrorism, it takes both skill and chance. RAND Rev 31(3):30
52. Johnson SC (1998) Psychological evaluation of theodore John Kaczynski. Federal Correctional Institution Butner, North Carolina
53. Kurtz H (1995) Unabomber manifesto is published: public safety reasons cited in joint decision by Post, NY Times. The Washington Post, 19 Sept, A01
54. Hoffman B (1998) Inside terrorism. Columbia University Press, New York
55. Laqueur W (1993) The uses and limits of intelligence. Transaction Publishers, Brunswick, NJ
56. Weimann G (2006) Terror on the internet. United States Institute of Peace Press, Washington, DC
57. Schwirtz M (2011) Norway's premier vows to keep an open society. The New York Times, 27 July
58. MacDougall I Ritter K (2011) Norway PM: attacks response to be 'more democracy', The Washington Times, 27 July
59. MacDougall I Ritter K (2011) Norway suspect also considered other targets. Denver Post, 31 July
60. Pogatchnik S (2011) Oslo bombing: Norway police's response to massacre criticized. Huffington Post, 6 Sept
61. Wildavsky A (1988) Searching for safety. Transaction Publishers, New Brunswick
62. Coaffee J (2006) From counterterrorism to resilience. The Eur Legacy 11(4):389–403
63. Furedi F (2007) Invitation to terror: the expanding empire of the unknown. Continuum, London
64. Bakker E, de Graaf B (2010) Lone wolves: how to prevent this phenomenon?. International Centre for Counter-Terrorism, The Hague
65. Schuster H, Stone C (2005) Hunting eric rudolph. Berkley Books, New York
66. Buncombe A (2000) 'Inspiration' came from Atlanta Olympics bomb. The Independent, 30 June
67. Clough S (2000) Bombings 'inspired by Atlanta attack'. The Daily Telegraph, 6 June
68. Demant F, Slootman M, Buijs F, Tillie J (2008) Decline and disengagement: an analysis of processes of deradicalisation. IMES, Universiteit van Amsterdam, Amsterdam
69. Wieviorka M (2003) The making of terrorism, 2nd edn. University of Chicago Press, Chicago
70. Brysk A (2007) Human rights and national insecurity. In: Brysk A, Shafir G (eds) National insecurity and human rights: democracies debate counterterrorism. University of California Press, Berkeley, pp 1–13

71. Geller A, Macdougall I (2011) Norway massacre forces new look at security in Europe. Denver Post, 5 August. http://www.denverpost.com/nationworld/ci_18620993. Accessed 7 Aug 2011
72. Christensen C (2004) Political victims and media focus: the killings of Laurent Kabila, Zoran Djindjic, Anna Lindh and Pim Fortuyn. J Crime Conflict Media 1(2):23–40

Chapter 9
Conclusion and Outlook

This volume set out to produce an in-depth understanding of lone wolf terrorism by analyzing six key dimensions of this phenomenon which cover multiple levels of analysis: the individual, family and interpersonal relations, group and social movement, state and government, past and present historical periods. These levels of analysis, which are closely intertwined, jointly shape lone wolf terrorism as we know it. On the basis of the preceding analysis, it is now possible to draw together and reflect on the main features, patterns and trends in lone wolf terrorism with due regard to both its idiosyncrasies and universalities.

The first conclusion to be drawn is that lone wolf terrorism is not a new phenomenon and dates back to at least the nineteenth century. This is an important point that places lone wolf terrorism in its historical context, and falsifies recent claims that lone wolves represent a "new paradigm" [1] or a "new terrorist threat" fuelled mainly by Internet propaganda [2]. Although the strategy of leaderless resistance principally developed from within the radical right from the 1970s onwards, it has been advocated and used by a variety of militant actors across space and time. The close historical association between leaderless resistance and America's radical right is nevertheless key to understanding the geography of lone wolf terrorist attacks, especially their relative prevalence among right-wing extremists, White supremacists and radical anti-abortion activists in the United States.

Clearly, this emphasis on continuity as a central feature of lone wolf terrorism does not mean that nothing has changed. The overall incidence of lone wolf terrorism has been on the increase in recent decades in the 15 countries under study, from 30 identified attacks in the 1970s to 73 in the 2000s.[12] The most marked increase in lone wolf terrorism took place in the European countries in the research sample, where the total number of attacks quadrupled between the 1970s and 2000s. How then can this increase be explained? Although there is no single explanation, a number of key contributing factors can be identified. First, lone wolf terrorist attacks

[12] These 15 countries are: United Kingdom, Germany, France, Spain, Italy, Poland, The Netherlands, Denmark, Sweden, Czech Republic, Portugal, Russia, Australia, Canada and United States. See Chap. 2 for more detail.

R. Spaaij, *Understanding Lone Wolf Terrorism*, SpringerBriefs in Criminology,
DOI: 10.1007/978-94-007-2981-0_9,

may be seen in part as the remnants of successfully combated and disrupted group-actor terrorism, with a number of extremist communities now advocating solo attacks which are often deemed less vulnerable to detection, infiltration and prosecution by the state. For example, in recent times Al Qaeda and related radical Islamist groups have encouraged lone wolf attacks as an effective strategy to strike against western targets. This call for individual jihad appears to have inspired, directly or indirectly, a number of lone wolf terrorist attacks in western countries.

A second explanation refers to the increased prevalence of the Internet as a vehicle through which to disseminate extreme ideologies. Indeed, the Internet can be an incubator or accelerator of lone wolf terrorism, enabling alienated individuals to make contact with communities of support and locate radical material. As Pantucci [3, p. 11] argues:

> The increasing prevalence of the internet and the easy availability of extremist material online have fostered the growth of the autodidactic extremist. The loner leaning towards violence can now easily teach himself the extremist creed, and then define his global outlook along the same lines, using it as a justification when carrying out an act of violence.

The Appendix describes several recent lone wolf terrorist incidents in which the Internet performed an enabling role through the easy accessibility of radical narratives and operational or emotional support. However, even though lone wolf terrorists might radicalize more easily or rapidly and be more aware of like-minded others because of their access to online information, it should be stressed that the Internet is not a *cause* of lone wolf terrorism. Lone wolf terrorists' attitudes and beliefs are shaped only in part by radical material or communities of support encountered online. Vicarious engagement with such material or communities is clearly not restricted to the Internet; in many cases it involves self-study of offline sources, such as radical literature and media accounts of specific terrorist incidents.

Finally, the methodological issues discussed in Chap. 2 should be taken into consideration when interpreting the development of lone wolf terrorism over time. There were significant gaps in the initial database of lone wolf terrorism compiled by the author in 2007 [4, 5], most of which have subsequently been resolved through the analysis of the Global Terrorism Database (GTD) and other open-source information. Nevertheless, some gaps and possible inconsistencies inevitably remain. There is likely to be a "hidden figure" of lone wolf terrorism unreported to/by the authorities or news media, particularly in historical periods and regions of the world with less media coverage. Differences in levels of lone wolf terrorist attacks over time may also be partially explained by variations in the data collection for the GTD [6], although, as discussed in Chap. 2, every effort was made to ensure the continuity of the lone wolf terrorism data between 1968 and 2010.[13]

---

[13] The GTD data collection "was done in real time for cases between 1970 and 1997, was retrospective between 1998 and 2007, and is again in real time after 2007" [6]. Some of the open sources used have since become unavailable, impeding efforts to collect a complete census of terrorist attacks between 1998 and 2007. However, given that the number of identified lone wolf terrorist attacks is actually *higher* after 1997 means that the differences in data collection cannot explain the observed increase over time.

translate theory into action varies significantly. As noted, there is often a disconnect between intention and capability, for example with regard to bomb-making and surveillance skills [14]. It is for this reason that many lone wolf terrorist attacks fail to claim any lives or only the life of the perpetrator. Nonetheless, lone wolves can learn and improve their skills through practice and experimentation. Furthermore, depending on the level of risk aversion, the discrepancy between intention and capability is likely to inform lone wolf terrorists' choice of targets and weapons. This may be one reason why firearms are the most common weapon used in lone wolf terrorist attacks, albeit that the preferred weapons of lone wolf terrorists vary across cultures (for reasons discussed in Chap. 7). Lone wolf terrorists principally target civilians; however, government officials and politicians are also relatively frequently targeted. Most targets at some level symbolize the perceived righteousness of the terrorist's cause and the perceived evil of the enemy. Where enhanced security limits lone wolf terrorists' access to intended targets, they may instead attack soft targets that also fit into the (often loosely defined) category of "the enemy".

It is essential, then, that counterterrorism operations to target lone wolf terrorism be informed by the specific context within which it occurs, including the nature and ends of the actors resorting to terrorist violence and the breadth and depth of their support. Notwithstanding this context specificity, it is possible to identify some key commonalities in government and community responses to acts of lone wolf terrorism. A broad strategy focused on a combination of interdiction, prevention, intelligence gathering by means of interpersonal contact, counter-radicalization, emergency preparedness and resilience appears to be an effective approach to minimizing lone wolf terrorism and its impact [15]. Although in some cases short-term conciliation efforts have been undertaken, long-term conciliatory responses aimed at mitigating some of the underlying grievances and preventing violent radicalization generally remain undervalued and deserve further attention. Law enforcement of course plays a central role in efforts to combat lone wolf terrorism, ranging from reactive policing (e.g. criminal investigation) to proactive policing (security intelligence). However, the exact impact of counterterrorism measures on lone wolf terrorism remains underexplored, most notably in relation to the possible link between effective repressive actions against group-actor terrorism and the increase in lone wolf terrorist attacks.

Notwithstanding the pivotal nature of counterterrorism measures in combating lone wolf terrorism, it is imperative that responses to lone wolf terrorism be based on democratic principles and respect for human rights, and adequate safeguards need to be built in to prevent further erosion of civil liberties as much as possible. Although the efficacy of democratic responses is often dismissed by those who advocate repressive coercion, democracy is actually the best basis for a long-term response to terrorism in liberal democratic societies [16–18].

It should be reiterated here that acts of lone wolf terrorism cannot always be prevented, and these acts clearly do have shocking, painful and costly ramifications, particularly for the families and friends of the victims. However, what is also clear is that in the long term these acts of terrorism neither seriously threaten the integrity of society, nor fundamentally undermine the way of life of a nation or community. In the final analysis, then, the possibility of a lone wolf terrorist attack should be viewed as a manageable risk among many other risks that liberal democratic societies face, and in the event such an attack takes place, communities can, and will, bounce back.

References

1. Boston W (2011) Norway attacks: the worrying rise of the lone-wolf terrorist. Time, 28 July. http://www.time.com/time/world/article/0,8599,2085658,00.html#ixzz1YS3iZyYd. Accessed 12 Aug 2011
2. Rising D (2011) Lone wolf has become new terrorist threat. Star Tribune, 5 September. http://www.startribune.com/nation/129242863.html?page=1&c=y. Accessed 14 Sept 2011
3. Pantucci R (2011) A typology of lone wolves: preliminary analysis of lone Islamist terrorists. ICSR, London
4. Spaaij R (2007) Lone-wolf terrorism. Report for the European Commission Sixth Framework program Transnational Terrorism, Security and the Rule of Law. COT Institute for Safety, Security and Crisis Management, The Hague
5. Spaaij R (2010) The enigma of lone wolf terrorism: an assessment. Stud Conflict Terrorism 33(9):854–870
6. Global Terrorism Database (2011) Data collection methodology. http://www.start.umd.edu/gtd/using-gtd/. Accessed 12 Aug 2011
7. Enders W, Sandler T (2005) After 9/11: is it all different now? J Conflict Resolut 49(2):259–277
8. Stern J (2003) Terror in the name of God: why religious militants kill. HarperCollins, New York
9. Horgan J (2005) The psychology of terrorism. Routledge, London
10. Borum R (2012) Psychology of terrorism. In: Christie DJ (ed) Encyclopedia of peace psychology. Wiley, Malden
11. Hewitt C (2003) Understanding terrorism in America: from the Klan to Al Qaeda. Routledge, New York
12. Juergensmeyer M (2000) Terror in the mind of God: the global rise of religious violence. University of California Press, Berkeley
13. Jackson P (2011) Solo actor terrorism and the mythology of the lone wolf. In: Gable G, Jackson P (eds) Lone wolves: myth or reality?. Searchlight, Ilford, pp 79–88
14. Stewart S, Burton F (2008) Lone wolf lessons. STRATFOR global intelligence. http://www.stratfor.com/weekly/20090603_lone_wolf_lessons. Accessed 4 Nov 2010
15. Bakker E, de Graaf B (2010) A lone wolves: how to prevent this phenomenon?. International Centre for Counter-Terrorism, The Hague
16. Sederberg PC (2003) Global terrorism: problems of challenge and response. In: Kegley CW Jr (ed) The new global terrorism: characteristics, causes, controls. Prentice Hall, Upper Saddle River, pp 267–284
17. Wilkinson P (2006) Terrorism versus democracy: the liberal state response, 2nd edn. Routledge, London
18. Brysk A (2007) Human rights and national insecurity. In: Brysk A, Shafir G (eds) National insecurity and human rights: democracies debate counterterrorism. University of California Press, Berkeley, pp 1–13

Appendix: Chronology of Lone Wolf Terrorism in 15 Countries, 1968–2010

Year	Country	Fatalities	Injuries	Description
1968	United States	1	5	Assassination of Senator Robert F. Kennedy in Los Angeles. Five bystanders are wounded. The Palestinian-born perpetrator, Sirhan Sirhan, wrote in his diary that he hated Kennedy because of his support for Israel and his pledge to give jet bombers to Israel. Some investigators question the validity of the official story that casts Sirhan as a lone wolf.
1970	France	0	0	A TWA 707 flight en route from Paris to Rome with 20 persons on board is hijacked by Frenchman Christian Belon, who is armed with a pistol. He states that he wanted to spite Americans and Israelis for their aggression in the Middle East.
1970	Italy	0	0	An Alitalia DC-9 flying from Genoa to Rome is hijacked by a young Italian man armed with a toy pistol. The plane is diverted to Cairo. Thirty-five passengers are taken hostage, reportedly in protest of the Middle East conflict.
1972	Germany	1	0	An Air Canada DC-8 scheduled to fly from Frankfurt to Montreal and Toronto is hijacked on the ground by an armed gunman, Viktor Widera, who forces everybody off the plane except one stewardess whom he holds hostage for 24 hours. Widera demands the release of a Czech national being held by West Germany for hijacking an aircraft from Prague to Nuremburg, as well as the release of several other Czechs. Police eventually shoot and kill the hijacker aboard the aircraft.
1972–1973	United States	10	13	Black militant Mark Essex carries out two shooting incidents in New Orleans. On New Year's Eve 1972 he shoots three police officers, killing two.

(continued)

R. Spaaij, *Understanding Lone Wolf Terrorism*, SpringerBriefs in Criminology,
DOI: 10.1007/978-94-007-2981-0, © The Author(s) 2012

(continued)

Year	Country	Fatalities	Injuries	Description
				On 7 January 1973, Essex shoots several people at a hotel in dowtown New Orleans. He is eventually shot and killed by police. A former US Navy sailor, Essex claimed to be the victim of the Navy's institutionalized racial discrimination and developed an intense hatred of White people and police officers.
1972–1975	United States	7	10+	White supremacist Neal Long carries out a series of shootings in Ohio between 1972 and 1975. His first shooting injured five Black men, on 31 July 1972. Long's attacks further include the murders of three Black males (on 26 September 1973, 3 July 1974 and 22 July 1974) and the assassination of Rev. William Wright, a Black minister who is killed by a shotgun blast in front of his church (12 May 1974). On 19 September 1975 Long shoots and kills desegregation planner Dr Charles Glatt at the old federal building in Dayton. Long is detained immediately after this shooting.
1973	France	1	0	A man armed with guns and grenades holds five people hostage at Calvi Airport on the island of Corsica after an aborted attempt to hijack an aircraft. The man is killed by police gunfire.
1973	United States	0	0	White supremacist Byron de la Beckwith is stopped and arrested by police for transporting a ticking bomb, which was reportedly meant to kill the regional director of the Anti-Defamation League, A.I. Botnick, in New Orleans.
1974	United States	3	35	Muharem Kurbegovic, a Yugoslavian-born engineer, carries out a series of bombings in Los Angeles. Kurbegovic detonates a bomb at Los Angeles International Airport, which kills three people and injures 35. Kurbegovic is also convicted for trying to bomb the Greyhound bus terminal in Los Angeles and for firebombing the homes of several government officials. Kurbe-govic acted alone and had no outside support; however, he claimed that he was a military officer of a fictitious group "Aliens of America". He is one of the first to threaten to release nerve agents in populated areas.
1976–1980	United States	18	7	White supremacist Joseph Paul Franklin carries out at least 16 shootings and bombings between 1976 and 1980, principally targeting African American men, "mixed-race" couples, Jews and civil rights activists in the United States. Franklin also shoots Hustler publisher Larry Flynt, leaving him paralyzed from the waist down. Although he acted alone, Franklin may have had connections with the Ku Klux Klan.

(continued)

(continued)

Year	Country	Fatalities	Injuries	Description
1977	Poland	0	0	Police are reported to have stopped an aircraft hijacking attempt at Krakow airport by a Polish man who seized a hostage and attempted to take over an aircraft ready for take-off to Nuremberg, West Germany. The perpetrator fires several shots before being overpowered by soldiers dressed as mechanics.
1977	Italy	0	0	The Lufthansa office in Genoa is firebombed, causing only minor damage. A left-wing student who is arrested and charged with the attack states that the attack was a protest against West Germany's policies concerning extremists.
1977	France	0	0	An Air France flight en route from Paris to Cairo via Nice is diverted by a lone Egyptian hijacker who claims to have dynamite. The aircraft eventually lands in Italy, where the hijacker is arrested. The perpetrator states that he seized the plane in an effort to bring Egypt and Libya together after the recent fighting between the two countries.
1978–1995	United States	3	23	Theodore Kaczynski, also known as the Unabomber, plants or mails 16 improvised explosive devices over a period of nearly 18 years, targeting scientists, technological experts and other civilians. His first bomb, in May 1978, targets Professor Buckley Crist at Northwestern University. For six years, between 1987 and 1993, Kaczynski remains inactive. In June 1993 he restarts his bomb campaign. His final attack comes on 24 April 1995, when a package bomb sent to the offices of the California Forestry Association kills the association's president.
1979	Australia	1	0	A bomb-wielding hijacker holding a knife to a woman's throat is critically wounded by police who overpower him inside a Pan American aircraft at Sydney's Mascot Airport.. An anti-hijack squad rescues the woman after her abductor snatches her from the customs hall of the airport terminal and forces her aboard the aircraft bound for Los Angeles. The hijacker, the Italian Dimiscus Sperantzo, later dies from his wounds. It is the first reported hijacking in Australia of an overseas aircraft.
1980	United States	5+ (possibly up to 13)	1+	White supremacist Joseph Christopher, 25, launches a one-man war against African American men in Buffalo and Niagara Falls, in September 1980. During a three-day killing spree, from 22 to 24 September 1980, four Black males are shot to death with a .22 caliber gun.

(continued)

(continued)

Year	Country	Fatalities	Injuries	Description
1980	Italy	0	0	A Tunisian hijacker holds 89 persons hostage on an Alitalia DC-9 flight for 12 hours, claiming he has an accomplice with a bomb. The 28-year-old hijacker demands that the passengers be exchanged in Tunisia for 25 jailed union leaders who must also be given back their jobs. He seizes the aircraft midway through its scheduled flight from Rome to Tunis. However, the airport where he wants the aircraft to be diverted to is closed due to a sand storm. The plane eventually lands in Palermo where, after a stalemate, the hijacker surrenders to Italian authorities.
1980	France	2	1	An unidentified man breaks into a travel agency in Paris and kills the owner and his wife and wounds his secretary. The owners of the agency are Egyptian-born Jews sympathetic to the Camp David Middle East peace accords. The attacker escapes, leaving behind his weapon.
1982	United States	3	1	Neo-Nazi Frank Spisak Jr. shoots and kills three Black males, including the Black minister Rev. Horace Rickerson in Cleveland, Ohio.
1982	United States	0	0	After threatening to blow up the Washington Monument, anti-nuclear weapons activist Norman Mayer is shot and killed by police after a ten-hour siege. The subsequent investigation discloses that Mayer did not have any explosives.
1982	Portugal	0	0	Juan María Fernández Krohn, a former Roman Catholic priest, tries to kill Pope John Paul II with a bayonet. He is sentenced to six years in prison for attempted murder. At his trial Fernández Krohn states that he acted because "the pontiff betrayed the church and encouraged communism through compromise with Soviet-Bloc countries". He is again arrested in 2000 after climbing over a security barricade at the Royal Palace of Brussels, reportedly intent on killing either Belgian King Albert II or the approaching Spanish King Juan Carlos.
1983	United States	0	0	Armed with a 9 mm submachine automatic rifle and possibly a bomb, Iranian immigrant, Hussein Shey Kholya, hijacks Rio Airways Flight 252 halfway through the one-hour flight from Killeen, Texas, en route to Dallas-Fort Worth Regional Airport in Dallas. During the incident, Kholya holds the 21 passengers and crew members hostage.

(continued)

(continued)

Year	Country	Fatalities	Injuries	Description
				He releases the hostages after having diverted the plane to Nuevo Laredo, Mexico. Kholya strikes a deal with Mexican authorities for a plane ticket to Cuba in exchange for the safe release of the passengers. All hostages are released unharmed. Kholya's avowed motive for the hijacking is his opposition to US foreign policy towards Iran.
1983	France	0	0	A 22-year-old Polish man fires at the Soviet Consulate, resulting in 13 bullet holes and a number of broken windows.
1983	USSR (Russia)	0	0	A man in his early thirties roars past Soviet guards outside the British Embassy in Moscow and drives a car containing a homemade bomb into the diplomatic compound. The Russian guards follow the man into the embassy courtyard and drag him out his car. The explosive device is safely removed.
1983	Spain	1	1	An employee of the Jordanian Embassy is killed and another seriously wounded by a single assailant who fires a submachine gun into their car on a street in Madrid. The attacker escapes after the attack.
1984	Spain	0	1	A gunman carrying a false Moroccan passport is arrested shortly after he shoots and wounds a Lebanese citizen in a shopping mall in the center of Madrid.
1984	France	2	3	A French citizen fires randomly into a cafe frequented by Turkish workers, killing two of them and wounding three others.
1984	Canada	3	29	A bomb explodes in a Montreal train station on Labor Day, killing three French tourists and injuring 29 others. Shortly after the bomb detonated, an anonymous caller warns police that a second bomb has been planted in the railroad station. A police search fails to locate a second bomb. A rambling, barely coherent note is given to police three days earlier by a ticket agent at the station. The letter threatens the life of the Pope who was due to visit Canada.
1985	Germany	0	0	The commander of Britain's Royal Air Force in West Germany is shot at by a passing motorist on the highway, but the assailant may have been firing blanks. Three shots are fired at the chauffeur-driven vehicle, but there is no sign of any bullets actually hitting the victim's car.
1985	Germany	0	0	A lone hijacker with a knife forces a Lufthansa aircraft en route to Athens from Munich to land at Istanbul's Yesilkoy Airport. Upon landing in Turkey the 142 passengers are released, and the man, believed to be a Libyan, demands the plane fly on to Libya. The man is eventually forced to surrender to the authorities.

(continued)

(continued)

Year	Country	Fatalities	Injuries	Description
1986	Netherlands	0	0	A man from Rotterdam is arrested in connection with an arson attack against a car belong-ing to the Soviet Embassy in The Hague. The car was parked near the embassy at the time of the attack. The man admits to having set the fire in protest against the Soviet occupation of Afghanistan. The attack is reportedly a one-man operation.
1988	Germany	0	0	Two Molotov cocktails are hurled at a US Army barracks in West Berlin by an unidentified man on a bicycle. The suspect escapes.
1988	Germany	0	0	An armed Lebanese man takes hostages at the Libyan Arab People's Bureau in Bonn, threatening to use force if he not be transported out of Germany. Eleven hours later the man is overpowered by German police.
1988	Canada	0	1	A 17-year-old Sikh shoots and seriously wounds the editor of a Punjabi-language newspaper in Vancouver.
1989	United States	2	0	Walter Leroy (Roy) Moody Jr. carries out a number of mail bomb attacks, killing Judge Robert Vance and civil rights attorney Robert Robinson. The same week, two more package bombs are intercepted en route to a federal courthouse and an office of the National Association for the Advancement of Colored People (NAACP) in Jacksonville, Florida. Both package bombs are disarmed. Moody is convicted on all counts.
1991	Germany	0	0	Three employees of a United States government agency are fired on and a grenade is tossed at the hotel in which they are staying in Berlin. A Lebanese man is later taken into custody in connection with the attack.
1991	Russia	1	0	A man in Leningrad tries to hijack a flight to Sweden. The man threatens the crew with an anti-tank grenade which detonates. The hijacker is killed in the attack.
1992	Canada	0	1	A Sudanese Islamist leader is injured when he and his advisors are attacked by an exiled martial arts expert at an airport in Ottawa.
1992–1993	United States	0	2	Anti-abortion activist Rachelle Shannon sets fire to a number of women's health and abortion clinics, using molotov cocktails and other types of incendiary device. She also shoots and wounds Dr George Tiller, an abortion provider in Wichita, Kansas.
1993	Sweden	0	0	A right-wing extremist fires at immigrants with a laser-sighted gun.
1993	France	0	0	An Algerian man armed with a knife attempts to hijack a domestic flight from Paris to Nice. He also claims to have an explosive device. Upon landing

(continued)

(continued)

Year	Country	Fatalities	Injuries	Description
				in Nice the hijacker demands that the flight continue on to Libya. The hijacker is eventually apprehended by police, and it is discovered that he does not have an explosive.
1993	United States	2	3	Pakistani immigrant Mir Aimal Kansi shoots five individuals working for the CIA outside CIA headquarters, killing two and injuring three others.
1993	United States	1	0	Anti-abortion activist Michael Griffin murders Dr David Gunn of Pensacola Medical Services, Florida. After shooting Dr Gunn in the back three times, Griffin surrenders to police, who were at the clinic to monitor an anti-abortion demonstration. Although Griffin acted alone, he may have been connected to the Army of God.
1993	United States	6	19	Black militant Colin Ferguson opens fire with a handgun on a crowded commuter train in New York. Six people are killed and 19 are wounded. All the victims are White or Asian. Handwritten notes found on Ferguson express his hatred of White and Asian people.
1994	United States	1	2	Lebanese-born immigrant Rashid Baz fires on a van carrying a group of Hasidic students in New York City, killing one and wounding two other students. At his trial, it is claimed that the attack is a response to the massacre of Muslim worshippers by a Jewish extremist in the Israeli-occupied West Bank a few days earlier.
1994	United States	2	1	Anti-abortion militant Paul Hill fatally shoots Dr John Britton in Pensacola, Florida. Britton's escort, June Barrett, is injured.
1994	United States	2	5	Anti-abortion activist John Salvi III kills two employees and injures five other employees of the Planned Parenthood of Greater Boston clinic and the Preterm Health Services clinic in two separate gun attacks in Massachusetts. The next day Salvi fires shots at the Norfolk's Hillcrest Clinic in Norfolk, Virginia. There are no casualties. Salvi is captured by authorities shortly after this incident.
1994–2006	Italy	0	10+	The "Italian Unabomber", whose identity remains unknown, appears to have planted up to 30 improvised explosive devices in consumer products, mainly food, between 1994 and 2006. Most explosive devices are left in public spaces such as beaches, cemeteries and churches. At least ten people have been injured by the bombs. In 2006 a 49-year-old engineer is charged with the bombings, but he is later acquitted due to lack of evidence.

(continued)

(continued)

Year	Country	Fatalities	Injuries	Description
1996	United States	2	10	White supremacist Larry Shoemake opens fire on a shopping center in an African American neighbourhood in Jackson, Mississippi, killing one person and wounding ten. Shoemake then dies in a fire. Notes left at his home suggest the attack was racially motivated.
1996–1998	United States	3	120+	Eric Rudolph carries out a number of bombing attacks in two states, Georgia and Alabama. His attacks include a bomb attack at Centennial Olympic Park during the 1996 Summer Olympics in Atlanta, killing one and injuring 111 other visitors. Rudolph also bombs two abortion clinics, on 16 January 1997 and 29 January 1998, and a gay and lesbian nightclub on 21 February 1997. In 2005 Eric Rudolph pleads guilty to these four attacks and is sentenced to life in prison.
1997	United States	2	6	Sixty-nine-year-old Palestinian male Ali Hasan Abu Kamal fires a gun into a crowd on the Empire State Building's 86th-floor observation deck, killing two (including the shooter) and injuring six others.
1998	United States	1	0	Radical Roman Catholic and anti-abortion activist James Kopp kills Dr Barnett Slepian, a doctor who legally performed abortions, by a single shot fired through the kitchen window of his home in Amherst, New York.
1998	United Kingdom	0	1	Police believe the "Mardi Gras bomber" is responsible for an explosion inside a man's car. The victim had picked up the improvised explosive device, which was hidden in a plastic bag, at a supermarket. The man is slightly injured.
1998	Spain	0	0	Javier Gomez hijacks a domestic Iberia flight en route from Seville to Barcelona. The hijacker claims to have an explosive device and requests that the plane be taken to Tel Aviv. It is later discovered that he was unarmed.
1999	United States	0	0	Frank Darwin Alexander carries out at least three bomb attacks. On 26 March 1999 he sends a mail bomb addressed to Bill Clinton to the White House. The device detonates in inside a truck trailer at the Washington DC bulk mail center. There are no casualties, but three mail containers are damaged. On 28 March 1999, Alexander sends a mail bomb addressed to John Hagee, a preacher with Cornerstone Ministries, in San Antonio. The device detonates at the Dallas bulk mail center. There are no casualties but machinery and equipment at the facility are damaged. On 29 March 1999 he sends a third mail bomb, addressed to the Bureau of Alcohol, Tobacco and Firearms office in Las Vegas. Alexander notifies

(continued)

(continued)

Year	Country	Fatalities	Injuries	Description
				authorities that the bomb is located at the Las Vegas Greyhound bus station and police subsequently disarm and remove the device.
1999	United States	1	5	White supremacist Buford Furrow opens fire in a Jewish community center in Granada Hills, California, wounding five people. Later that day, he shoots and kills a Filipino mailman. Furrow walks into the FBI office in Las Vegas the next morning and surrenders. He states that he "wanted to send a message to America by killing Jews".
1999	United Kingdom	3	129	David Copeland carries out a two-week bombing campaign targeting London's Black, Asian and gay communities. Over three successive weekends, Copeland places improvised explosive devices in public locations. The first bomb detonates outside a supermarket in Brixton, an area known for its large Black and minority ethnic population. The second bomb explodes just off Brick Lane, East London, which has a large South Asian community. The third and final bomb detonates in the busy Admiral Duncan pub in Soho, central London, a focal point for London's gay community. The attacks kill a total of three people, including a pregnant woman, and injure 129 others.
2000	Denmark	0	1	Boris Zhilko, a Russian diplomat, is injured when a bottle containing an incendiary mixture is thrown into the Russian Consular Office in Copenhagen. The perpetrator is detained and claims his attack on the embassy was a "response to Russia's actions in Chechnya".
2000	Germany	1	4	One woman is killed and four others injured—all immigrants from Eastern Europe—when a masked man fires shots on a beauty salon in Berlin. He then hurls a grenade into the shop and escapes. The shop is located in a heavily Russian-populated area of the city. Authorities believe that the attack is connected to another bomb attack against Russian immigrants in Düsseldorf in July 2000.
2000	United States	3	2	Black militant Ronald Taylor shoots five people, killing three of them, in two fast-food restaurants in Wilkinsburg, Pennsylvania. Police and FBI agents searching Taylor's apartment reportedly found writings referring to "White trash" and denouncing Asians, Italians and the news media.
2000	United States	5	1	In a shooting spree in Pittsburgh, Pennsylvania, White supremacist Richard Baumhammers kills five people: an African American male, a Jewish woman and three Asian men.

(continued)

(continued)

Year	Country	Fatalities	Injuries	Description
2001	United States	0	0	US Army veteran John Allen Muhammad fires shots at a synagogue in Tacoma, Washington. A year later, in October 2002, Muhammad, together with accomplice Lee Malvo, terrorizes the Washington DC area for more than three weeks in a series of sniper shootings, killing ten and wounding three people. Muhammad is convicted of terrorism for intentionally instilling fear throughout the Washington community.
2001	Spain	0	0	A masked man enters a post office in Hernani, plants a bomb and leaves. The device explodes but does not cause any injuries.
2001	Australia	1	0	An armed security guard at an abortion clinic in Melbourne, the Fertility Control Clinic, is shot and killed by a lone gunman. The gunman is subdued by two bystanders and subsequently arrested.
2002	Spain	0	2+	On 22 September 2003 an ex-member of the former Catalan separatist group, Terra Lliure, is arrested in connection with four attacks that took place in Barcelona in 2002. The police find a number of fake personal documents, stolen bank cards, an imitation handgun, a real handgun, an air rifle, documents and publications of a radical nature, a computer and disks in the suspect's home. During the first attack, on 4 May 2002, the man reportedly uses flammable liquid to set fire to a television and telephone connections booster station. On 13 May 2002, he allegedly plants a device made up of two camping-gas cylinders and several lead balls. The device explodes at an ATM machine, injuring two people. On 12 December 2002, a homemade bomb explodes in a Bacelona tax office, causing considerable damage to the interior. The device starts a fire that is extinguished by the fire brigade.
2002	Nether-lands	1	0	Dutch politician Pim Fortuyn is shot and killed after an interview at a radio station in Hilversum. In November 2002, Volkert van der Graaf admits to murdering Fortuyn. He states that he perpetrated the attack to protect Muslim immigrants and other "vulnerable" members of Dutch society. Van der Graaf is sentenced to 18 years in prison.
2002	Spain	0	0	An improvised explosive device is found at the People's Party (PP) offices in Sanxenxo. The national police arrest a 44-year-old man in connection with this attack, another device left at a PP office and an arson attack on a military lorry that was assisting in cleaning up the recent oil spill.

(continued)

(continued)

Year	Country	Fatalities	Injuries	Description
2002	United States	0	7	Between 3 and 7 May 2002, 21-year-old college student Luke Helder mails 18 pipe bombs in five Midwestern states, collectively causing seven injuries. Most of the explosives come with typewritten notes that bemoan the power of the government and threaten more attacks. On 7 May 2002, the FBI and Nevada state authorities arrest Helder, who confesses to being responsible for all of the bombs. In 2004 a federal judge finds Helder unfit to stand trial.
2002	United States	3	3	Hesham Mohamed Ali Hadayet, an Egyptian immigrant, opens gunfire at the El Al airline ticket counter at Los Angeles International Airport, killing two people and wounding three others. The gunman leaves a letter stating that he is angered by Israel's treatment of Palestinians. Hadayet is shot dead by an El Al security guard.
2002	United States	0	0	Apparently protesting the state of human rights in North Korea, South Korean-born US citizen Steve Kim fires pistol shots outside the United Nations headquarters in New York. He throws a handful of leaflets condemning North Korea in the air.
2003	United States	0	0	Dwight Watson, a tobacco farmer protesting cuts in tobacco subsidies and the government's treatment of Gulf War veterans, drives his tractor into a pond near the Lincoln Memorial, Washington DC, and threatens to detonate a bomb. He surrenders two days later. No explosives are found.
2003	United Kingdom	0	0	A 37-year-old Venezuelan citizen, Rahaman Alan Hazil Mohammed, is arrested at London Gatwick Airport after authorities find a live grenade in his luggage. Gatwick's north terminal is evacuated and closed while authorities dispose of the grenade. He is sentences to six years in prison.
2003	Germany	0	0	A 17-year-old Lebanese citizen hijacks a bus with around 15 people on board near Bremen. The hijacker carries a starter's pistol and claims that he also carries a chemical weapon. The perpetrator demands the release of four Al Qaeda operatives and praises the work of the 9/11 hijackers. No shots are fired and no one is injured. Though of Lebanese origin, the hijacker has been living in Germany for several years. Authorities believe the perpetrator acted on his own and was not part of any organized terrorist group.
2003	Germany	0	0	A 27-year-old Lebanese man hijacks a bus, holding eight people hostage, in Berlin. The hijacker, who has a knife, demands that Israel withdraw from the Palestinian territories. Police officers storm the bus; no one is injured.

(continued)

(continued)

Year	Country	Fatalities	Injuries	Description
2004	Italy	1	0	Moustafa Chaouki, a 35-year-old Moroccan man who has been living in Italy for over 15 years, blows himself up outside a McDonald's restaurant in Brescia. Investigators find a note, written by the bomber, protesting the war in Iraq but stating that he is not a member of Al Qaeda or any other terrorist group. In the note, Chaouki says he is acting in the name of Allah for the war in Iraq, which he believes punishes innocent people. Chaouki also criticizes Italy for being too friendly with the US and Israel.
2006	United States	0	9	22-year-old Iranian-born American citizen Mohammed Reza Taheri-azar drives a Jeep Cherokee into a crowd of students at the University of North Caro-lina at Chapel Hill, injuring nine people. He is reported to have acted alone and be religiously motivated.
2006	United States	1	5	Naveed Afzal Haq, a 30-year-old American man of Pakistani descent, opens fire in the offices of the Jewish Federation of Greater Seattle, killing one woman and wounding five others. He reportedly states: "I am a Muslim American, angry at Israel" and "I'm not upset at people, I'm upset at your foreign policy".
2007	United States	0	0	An improvised explosive device hidden in a soft-side insulated cooler is found and defused in the parking lot of the Austin Women's Health Center, an abortion clinic in Austin, Texas. The potassium nitrate bomb contains 910 g of nails, a 12-inch piece of copper pipe, a mechanical timer and a propane cylinder. Anti-abortion activist Paul Ross Evans, 27, is found guilty and sentenced to 40 years in federal prison.
2008	United Kingdom	0	0	Forty-three-year-old neo-Nazi Neil Lewington is accused of planning terrorist attacks after being found with two explosive devices at a rail station in Lowestoft, Suffolk. Lewington reportedly wanted to emulate the Oklahoma City bomber, Timothy McVeigh, and the Soho nail bomber, David Copeland, and kept videos detailing their attacks at his home. Police discovers a bomb factory and other incriminating evidence in his bedroom. On 8 September 2009, Lewington is jailed for planning a racist bombing attack.
2009	Italy	0	2	Libyan citizen Mohamed Game injures himself and a paramilitary police officer when he throws an improvised explosive device made with fertilizer at the paramilitary police barracks in Milan. Game is reportedly opposed to Italy's military mission in Afghanistan. The media report that he shouted "Out of Afghanistan" before setting off the device.

(continued)

(continued)

Year	Country	Fatalities	Injuries	Description
2009	United States	1	0	Fifty-one-year-old anti-abortion activist Scott Roeder shoots and kills Dr George Tiller, an abortion provider, in the foyer of the Reformation Lutheran Church in Wichita, Kansas. Roeder is sentenced to life in prison.
2009	United States	1	1	Twenty-three-year-old African American Abdulhakim Mujahid Muhammad, who had changed his name from Carlos Leon Bledsoe after he converted to Islam, opens fire with a rifle on soldiers in front of a United States military recruiting office in Little Rock, Arkansas. He kills one soldier and wounds another. After his arrest, Muhammad acknowledges shooting the men. He reportedly tells police that he intended to kill as many Army personnel as possible and that he was angry at the US Army because of their attacks against Muslims overseas.
2009	United States	13	43	At the military base of Fort Hood, Texas, Major Nidal Malik Hasan opens fire on fellow soldiers with two semiautomatic guns, killing 13 and wounding 43 others. Military police forces shoot the gunman, a military psychiatrist who is believed to be a recent convert to Islam who opposes the wars in Iraq and Afghanistan.
2009	United States	0	2	Would-be suicide bomber Umar Farouk Abdulmutallab, a 23-year-old Nigerian national, detonates an explosive device that is attached to his body while on board of Northwest Flight 253 from Amsterdam to Detroit. The explosives are sewn into his underwear. The assailant and one passanger are wounded, and the aircraft is damaged. There have been some suggestions that the perpetrator is connected to Al Qaeda, however to date there is no conclusive evidence that verifies this claim.
2009–2010	Sweden	1+	7+	Thirty-eight-year-old Swedish citizen Peter Mangs is charged with one murder and five attempted murders following more than a series of "race-related" shootings between October 2009 and 2010 in Malmo. One victims is killed and at least seven are injured. Police suspect that Mangs is responsible for at least another three suspected murders.
2010	United Kingdom	0	1	Twenty-one-year-old student Roshonara Choudhry attempts to murder British Member of Parliament Stephen Timms outside Mr Timms' constituency surgery in East London. She repeatedly stabs her victim in the stomach with a three-inch kitchen knife. Choudhry is immediately captured and

(continued)

(continued)

Year	Country	Fatalities	Injuries	Description
				readily confesses her intention to police, stating that she targeted Mr Timms because of his strong support for the war in Iraq. Choudhry appears to have been driven by the ideology offered by Al Qaeda. She is convicted to life in prison.
2010	Sweden	1	2	Taimour Abdulwahab al-Abdaly, a 28-year-old Iraqi-born Swedish citizen, blows himself up and injures two others in an attempt to target Christmas shoppers in Stockholm. The first explosion comes from gas canisters in his car, and the second follows minutes later, when one of 12 pipe bombs strapped to him explodes, possibly prematurely. Minutes before the blasts, al-Abdaly sends recordings to the Swedish police and news media apologizing to his wife and young family. He also vows revenge in the name of Islam on Sweden for its participation in the war in Afghanistan and for cartoons published by a Swedish artist depicting the prophet Muhammad in an unflattering light. Al-Abdaly was a British university graduate who had been living in England until two weeks before the attack. Although the Swedish authorities believe that al-Abdaly acted alone, there have been some hints that he may have had some assistance. In March 2011 Scottish police arrest and charge Ezedden Khalid Ahmed al-Khaledi, a 30-year-old nursing student, with helping fund the suicide bomb attack.
2010	United States	2	13	Fifty-three-year-old Joseph Stack flies his private plane into the Internal Revenue Service (IRS) building in Austin, Texas, igniting a fire throughout the seven-story building. He is proclaimed dead on impact. Several workers are wounded and one IRS employe is killed. The building is destroyed. Stack posts an anti-government note on the Internet prior to the attack.

A Note on Sources

A detailed discussion of the research methodology is provided in Chap. 2. This chronology is an expanded and fully revised version of the database compiled by the author in 2007 for the European Commission Sixth Framework Program research project *Transnational Terrorism, Security and the Rule of Law* [1, 2]. The 15 countries included in the database are: United Kingdom, Germany, France, Spain, Italy, Poland, The Netherlands, Denmark, Sweden, Czech Republic, Portugal, Russia, Australia, Canada and United States. The majority of incidents listed in the Appendix are derived from the Global Terrorism Database (1968–2010) and the RAND-MIPT Terrorism Knowledge Base (1968–2007). Descriptions are also drawn from open sources such as media reports, security reports, academic treatises, and chronologies and encyclopedias of terrorism. Key open sources include: Hewitt [3, 4]; Kushner [5]; Mickolus [6]; Branum [7]; Pantucci [8]; Simon [9] (on Muharem Kurbegovic); Martin [10] (on Richard Baumhammers, Theodore Kaczynski and Eric Rudolph); Jenkins [11] (on Roy Moody); Juergensmeyer [12] (on Paul Hill and Eric Rudolph); Roth and Dolan [13] (on Steve Kim); *The New York Times*; *The Washington Post*; *The Times*; *The Guardian*; *La Repubblica*; *Corriere della Sera*; *Frankfurter Allgemeine*; *Le Monde*; *El País*; and *NRC Handelsblad*, among others. The chronology excludes: (1) attacks that are carried out by couples or trios (see Chap. 3); (2) attacks which lack a political aim (see Chap. 2); and (3) attacks that are perpetrated by an individual who is (presumably) a member of a terrorist group (see Chap. 2). The latter category includes for example Gordon Kahl, who killed two US Marshals on 13 February 1983, and Fran Stephanie Trutt, who attempted to murder corporate executive Leon Hirsch, on 10 November 1988. Please see Chap. 2 for more detail.

R. Spaaij, *Understanding Lone Wolf Terrorism*, SpringerBriefs in Criminology,
DOI: 10.1007/978-94-007-2981-0, © The Author(s) 2012

References

1. Spaaij R (2007) Lone-wolf terrorism. Report for the European Commission Sixth Framework program Transnational Terrorism, Security and the Rule of Law. COT Institute for Safety, Security and Crisis Management, The Hague
2. Spaaij R (2010) The enigma of lone wolf terrorism: an assessment. Stud Confl Terror 33(9):854–870
3. Hewitt C (2003) Understanding terrorism in America: from the Klan to al Qaeda. Routledge, New York
4. Hewitt C (2005) Political violence and terrorism in modern America. Praeger Security International, Westport
5. Kushner H (2003) Encyclopedia of terrorism. Sage, Thousand Oaks
6. Mickolus EF (1980) Transnational terrorism: a chronology of events, 1968–1979. Greenwood Press, Westport
7. Branum TL (2001) Aviation security in the new century. Federalist Society for Law and Public Policy Studies, Washington
8. Pantucci R (2011) A typology of lone wolves: preliminary analysis of lone Islamist terrorists. ICSR, London
9. Simon JD (2000) The alphabet bomber. In: Tucker JB (ed) Toxic terror: assessing terrorist use of chemical and biological weapons. MIT Press, Cambridge, pp 71–94
10. Martin G (2003) Understanding terrorism: challenges perspectives, and issues. Sage, Thousands Oaks
11. Jenkins R (1997) Blind vengeance: the Roy Moody mail bomb murders. University of Georgia Press, Atlanta
12. Juergensmeyer M (2000) Terror in the mind of God: the global rise of religious violence. University of California Press, Berkeley
13. Roth R, Dolan L (2002) Shots at UN narrowly miss employees. CNN, 3 Oct. http://archives.cnn.com/2002/US/Northeast/10/03/un.shots.fired/index.html. Accessed 14 June 2007

About the Author

Ramón Spaaij, PhD, is a Senior Research Fellow in the School of Social Sciences at La Trobe University, Australia, and the Amsterdam Institute for Social Science Research, University of Amsterdam, The Netherlands. He has lectured at several universities in sociology and conflict studies. Spaaij's main research expertise is in the sociology of sport, social inequalities, and terrorism and political violence. Spaaij has published on various aspects of terrorism and counterterrorism in books, articles and reports. He has published nine books including recent titles such as *Sport and Social Mobility: Crossing Boundaries* (Routledge 2011) and *The Social Impact of Sport: Cross-Cultural Perspectives* (Routledge 2010). His work has appeared in academic journals such as *International Sociology*, *Acta Sociologica*, *Journal of Sociology*, *Ethnic and Racial Studies*, *Studies in Conflict & Terrorism*, *Media International Australia*, *Journal of Sport and Social Issues* and *International Review for the Sociology of Sport*.

R. Spaaij, *Understanding Lone Wolf Terrorism*, SpringerBriefs in Criminology,
DOI: 10.1007/978-94-007-2981-0, © The Author(s) 2012

CPSIA information can be obtained at www.ICGtesting.com
Printed in the USA
LVOW100805130313

323981LV00002B/78/P